Phosphate
Fluorides
Toxic Torts

By

Gary O. Pittman

Phosphate Fluorides Toxic Torts

Published by Lulu.com

First Printing

ISBN: **978-0-615-49040-3**

Dedicated to my Co-workers

Special thanks to Anita M Knight & Carol Kopf & Richard Gentle

For proof reading

Cover Design, Editing & Compilation – George C Glasser

Introduction

George C. Glasser

When Gary Pittman contacted me about doing the editing on a book he wanted to write about his toxic tort litigation against Occidental Chemical Company back in the 1990s, I jumped at the chance.

Almost thirteen years before, I wrote several articles about the case and personally knew some of the people involved. Those articles were the highlight of my writing career.

Gary told me that he recently went to the doctor. The prognosis was that he's experiencing the first stages of dementia. He said the he felt that it was important to put his story in writing so other people might benefit from his experiences.

He first contacted me back in 1997 after reading several investigative exposés I wrote about the Florida phosphate fertilizer industry.

As it turned out, Gary was a long time employee at Occidental Chemical Corporation's (Oxychem) phosphate mining and processing operations in northern Florida. He and some other co-workers became seriously ill from exposure to the toxic emissions given off by the process and toxic chemicals used for processing phosphoric acid.

They were embroiled in toxic tort litigation with Occidental at the time, and Gary was just asking me a few questions about what I came across in my research that could help out with the case.

When he told me about the work environment and the adverse health effects he and the people in the toxic tort case suffered from, I instantly recognized that the symptoms were all related to exposures to toxic substances found in phosphoric acid production.

Gary was a godsend because I had one more article to write in the series I was doing, and I was looking for a new angle. However, as far as my research was going, I hit a brick wall and needed somebody on the inside.

Previously, my contacts were mostly scientists and toxicologists who knew little or nothing about the working conditions and the inner workings of the phosphate fertilizer industry.

I wanted to do something more gritty and from the proverbial 'horse's mouth.'

I liked Gary right away, mainly because unlike most of the people who contacted me, he wasn't pushing or begging me to write an article about his problems in hopes of getting a little attention. He wasn't one of what I coined, "The Professional Victims." Gary just wanted information to help beef-up his toxic tort case against Occidental, and we both knew that we had something to offer one another.

From the onset of our relationship, I wanted to write an article about Gary and his co-workers' lawsuit.

I did a lot of legal research, because, as an investigative environmental journalist, I had to learn about toxic tort litigation. It was just part of the game, and Gary's situation was just what I was interested in covering.

I knew that the article would be a good vehicle to use some of the legal knowledge I gained and give my readers a different perspective. It was a switch from the toxicologists' hypotheses of what may happen to the reality of 'what will happen.'

From what Gary shared with me, I knew it was one of those stories that might only come along once in a writer's career, and I wanted to be the person to write it.

Several years before, I purchased what then was the definitive toxic tort litigation guide – the five-volume set of the *"Law of Toxic Torts"* by Michael Dore and read the whole thing. Consequently, I knew that Gary and his co-workers were facing almost insurmountable odds.

I reviewed hundreds of cases, and gained insights into the corporate culture and their executives' sociopathic nature when it came to protecting "the company."

Often, corporations would spend more money on legal fees defending toxic tort cases than they would have spent settling with the plaintiffs in nondisclosure compensation agreements. Instead, corporation representatives proclaim their unequivocal innocence and the absolute safety of their operations. It was all so they could maintain the status quo.

I got an intimate picture of how a corporation and its management could be almost philanthropic to a fault and simultaneously poison whole communities without the slightest hesitation if it meant increasing profits.

From personal experience and observation, I knew the people who ran corporations inevitably shut down a factory or would lay-off a work force just before Christmas. It was just because some compulsive neurotic, corporate bean counter had to balance the books as if one more month's losses would make any difference to anybody other than the shareholders.

Then the management would get their bonus checks and engage in mutual backslapping sessions at the company Christmas party congratulating each other for another hatchet job well done.

I knew the sociopathic mindset and unscrupulous tactics of the machine Gary and his co-workers were facing in their fight for compensation, and they needed all the help they could get.

I also knew that Occidental was no stranger to litigation. In fact, they were the parent corporation of Hooker Chemical Corporation, which the defendants in the largest environmental litigation case ever brought against a corporation by the US Department of Justice on behalf of Environmental Protection Agency in US history.

It was the infamous "Love Canal" case in the early 1980s. Hooker Chemical Company, over a period of years, dumped 166,000 tons of toxic waste was in a New York landfill. Later, a school and 100 homes were built on and around the site. Heavy rains released the toxic chemical waste which led to a public health emergency. Hooker Chemical was found negligent in their disposal of waste. They paid out over 200 million dollars to the US government for clean-up costs.

Occidental Chemical, along with the usual suspects, produced the dioxin-laced defoliant Agent Orange supplied to the military during the Vietnam War.

Agent Orange was sprayed from airplanes over the jungles of Vietnam. The lawsuit was about illnesses and birth defects caused by the dioxins inherent to the product.

At the time, they were fighting a class action case about Agent Orange along with a few other smaller toxic tort cases.

Then, not only was Gary going up against a powerful Global corporation, he was essentially in a fight with the Florida phosphate industry, which at that time supplied 75% of the US supply and 25% of the World supply of phosphate fertilizer.

In Florida, along with the citrus and sugar industries, the phosphate industry rules the roost. Generally, a Florida court will rule in favor of the phosphate industry every time – it's all bought and paid for, and the little guy doesn't stand much of a chance.

Then there was a national security issue involved. Florida phosphate rock contains uranium oxide which was the largest source of yellow cake uranium for the nuclear industry in the US.

Central Florida's phosphate rock contains the largest reserves of Uranium the US, approximately one million metric tons.

Interestingly, a little known fact is that the source of much of the uranium that went into the making of the first atomic bombs came from phosphate mined in Central Florida's 'Bone Valley' region.

Lastly, the pollution scrubber liquor from processing the phosphate rock, Fluorosilicic acid was and still is added to about 75% of US cities that fluoridated drinking water. Saying anything that could be detrimental to that purported 'public health' practice, and the American Dental Association and The US Centers for Disease Control and Prevention (CDC) would be after you like a pack of rabid dogs.

I also was very familiar with the law firm defending Occidental, Holland and Knight. As far as ethics go, I heard enough stories from plaintiffs to know that they would go to any lengths in the defense of their clients. Gary, his attorneys, and co-workers were tangling with some of the nastiest defense lawyers in the business.

Holland and Knight have a Global reach and its foundation and reputation was built on their relationship with the Florida citrus and phosphate fertilizer industries.

That law firm was not a neophyte when it came to defending clients in toxic tort cases.

In my estimation, Gary and his co-plaintiffs didn't stand much of a chance, and I wanted to offer some help other than just exchanging information.

Back then, I had a lot of international contacts among the environmental activists' network who circulated my articles on the Internet. I also knew of several well-respected environmental periodicals with an international readership. I was sure they would snap up the story.

I knew I could get the story published with no problem and attract attention to the case.

The problem I foresaw with stories of that nature was that most of the people I wrote about would get cold feet and back out at the last minute leaving me with an article I spent months researching just sitting on the shelf and collecting dust.

After feeling Gary out for a few months, I popped the question to him about writing the article, and he said, "Why not….we don't have anything to lose."

He told me that several articles had already appeared in the local newspaper, and they needed all the publicity they could get.

I knew that I could give him a lot more than a short-lived newspaper article in the newspaper. My network of Internet contacts led to even more contacts. I saw my articles spread like wildfire among the environmental

Internet network, and even environmental and natural health magazines plucked them off the Internet and republished them in print.

Back then, the periodicals I regularly contributed material to had large international followings. I knew this story would have running shoes and last a long time – it wasn't going to be one of those 'newspaper headlines today, fish wrappers tomorrow stories.'

What I didn't realize at the time is the impact it would have, how far it would go, and to whom – and for how long it would stay in circulation.

The original print story that appeared in the editions of 1999 Winter/Spring edition of *"Earth Island Journal"* is still in circulation today on the Internet and became part of recommended reading for students studying environmental law and toxicology. The last it appeared in print was 2008 - 9 years after it was first published.

When the article first came out, the story even caused a stir at the USEPA and Agency for Toxic Substances and Disease Registry. Shortly after publication, the USEPA decided to review phosphate emission laws and tightened the regulations – but that all went away during the Bush/Cheney administration.

That article and the changes it caused would have never happened if it weren't for that group of people who had the courage to speak out and tell their stories. I simply reported it.

Later, I wrote an article that included personal accounts from the key people involved in the lawsuit and their wives. In my estimation, it was the best article I ever wrote, but I had difficulty in getting it published because editors said, 'It's just too bleak for our readership.'

Gary Pittman was the driving force behind the lawsuit. He invested thousands of dollars in the case and pressed forward in spite of his serious health problems, seeing his friends die, and facing the many other obstacles he encountered along the way.

When Gary contacted me and asked if I would help him with this book about the case, I was delighted to help because I always hoped he would write something from his personal perspective.

Did Gary win - yes and no. If you have your health, you can always make more money, but when you're poisoned and debilitated, you can never get enough money to buy back your health and sense of wellbeing.

For anyone thinking about toxic tort litigation or is involved with a case, this book chronicles a seven-year fight from an individual's perspective and is a must read.

- Ends -

Oxychem (Occidental Chemical Corporation)
in North Florida

Background

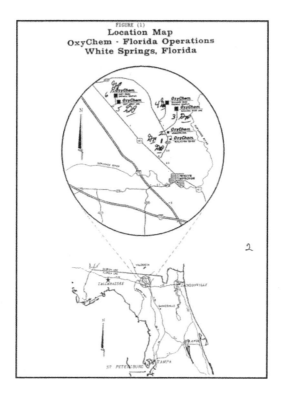

FIGURE (1)
Location Map
OxyChem · Florida Operations
White Springs, Florida

Although in Central Florida's "Bone Valley region, phosphate mining was a booming industry, it did not come to north Florida in a significant way until the 1960s when Occidental Petroleum Company's division Occidental Chemical Corporation (Oxychem) decided to diversify into the profitable fertilizer industry.

Long established companies already owned the Central Florida phosphate-mining district; however, the north Florida phosphate reserves were close enough to the surface to be economically feasible to mine.

Occidental took advantage of the opportunity and opened a mine in White Springs where it mined phosphate until 1995, when the Potash Corporation of Saskatchewan (PCS) purchased the operation.

---

* See Appendix: *Occidental Exposures: Gary's Story.*

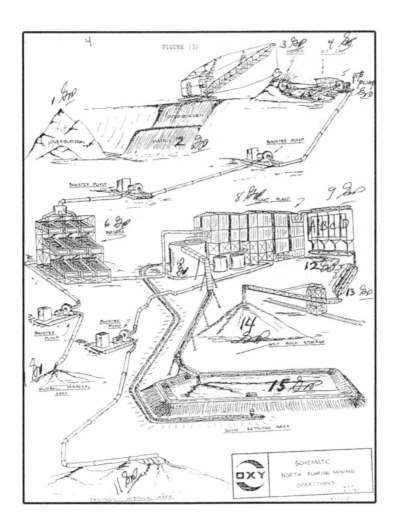

FIGURE (3)

SCHEMATIC
NORTH FLORIDA MINING
OPERATIONS

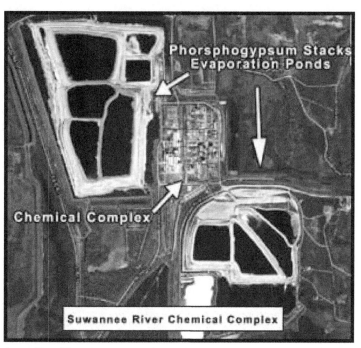

Phorsphogypsum Stacks
Evaporation Ponds

Chemical Complex

Suwannee River Chemical Complex

Phosphate Fertilizer Industry Overview

Rock phosphate is not an actual mineral because it has no definite chemical composition. It is a secondary deposit formed due to the accumulation of organic remains, mainly fossilized marine animal bones, where the part of the calcium is replaced by phosphorous, fluorine, and other minerals found in seawater, thus creating calcium phosphate more commonly called fluorapatite. The rock phosphate is usually found as phosphate nodules.

Due to its chemical properties, phosphate rock may contain significant quantities of naturally occurring radioactive materials (NORM):

- uranium (and its decay products, including radium)

- thorium (and its decay products)

Uranium concentrations in phosphate ores found in the U.S. range from 20 to 300 parts per million (ppm).

The most important use of phosphate rock is in the production of phosphate fertilizers. It accounted for over 90 percent of the phosphate rock demand in the United States in 2006.

Before phosphate ore is turned into fertilizer or other products, it is transformed into either phosphoric acid (through the wet process), or elemental phosphorus (through the thermal process). This processing concentrates NORM in the waste products, transforming them into

TENORM (Technologically-Enhanced Naturally-Occurring Radioactive Materials).

During the wet process, radionuclides present in the phosphate ore are selectively separated and concentrated. Around 80 percent of the radium-226 becomes concentrated in the phosphogypsum.

Phosphogypsum consists primarily of calcium sulfate dihydrate with small amounts of silica, usually as quartz, and unreacted phosphate rock. Radium and uranium, as well as minor amounts of USEPA toxic metals: Arsenic, barium, cadmium, chromium, lead, mercury, selenium, aluminum, silver, and high concentrations of fluorides are also present in phosphogypsum and its pore water. *(Edited from USEPA Fact Sheet)*

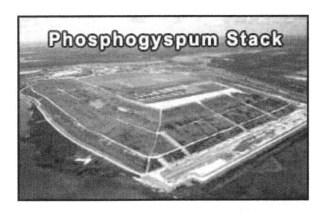

Oxychem Phosphoric Acid Complex - White Springs, Florida

Sarasota Herald-Tribune - 6 Feb 1997

Plant workers say chemicals mac

The three men say they were exposed to dozens of toxins on the job, and now suffer from conditions similar to Gulf war syndrome.

By Lebron Miles
NYT REGIONAL NEWSPAPERS

LAKE CITY — One current and two former workers at the area's largest private employer have filed workers' compensation claims, saying long-term chemical exposure has physically and mentally damaged them.

Occidental Chemical Corp. and PCS Phosphate have been named in two separate workers' compensation claims filed with state Department of Labor and Employment Security offices in Gainesville and Jacksonville.

The three men — Jesse Nash of Lake City, Gary Pittman of Jennings and Clinton Vann of Live Oak — say exposure to chemicals used to man-

ufacture phosphoric acid and other products at the White Springs plant is to blame for a variety of illnesses and their inability to continue to work.

"I intend to fight these people down to the wire," Pittman said. "And I'm not a fighter at heart, but now it's a mission."

Nash's claim is against both Occidental and PCS Phosphate, because he worked for both companies during his 18-year tenure in the plant's shipping department. PCS Phosphate bought Occidental's operation Oct. 31, 1995.

Nash still is employed by PCS Phosphate, but he has been on medical leave since July 3, 1996.

Pittman and Vann worked solely

for Occidental, and their claims have been consolidated. All three men are being represented by Ocala attorney Dorothy Clay Sims.

Pittman, a former supervisor at the plant, is on long-term disability since leaving work in May 1993. He worked for Occidental for 21 years. Vann, who mostly worked in the laboratory during his 27 years at Occidental, left the plant in February 1993 and is also on disability.

The men say they suffer from severe muscle weakness, fatigue, irregular heartbeats, memory loss, confusion, swelling in their joints, respiratory problems and headaches. They compare their symptoms to the Persian Gulf war syndrome affecting U.S. soldiers who served in Operation Desert Storm. Some believe the soldiers were exposed to chemical weapons agents during the war with Iraq.

Nash, Pittman and Vann say that in their combined years at the plant they were exposed to more than 100

Gainesville Sun - 7 Feb 1997

Chemical exposure blamed for illnesses

By LEBRON MILES
NYT Regional Newspapers

LAKE CITY — One current and two former workers at the area's largest private employer have filed workers' compensation claims, saying long-term chemical exposure has physically and mentally damaged them.

Occidental Chemical Corp. and PCS Phosphate have been named in two separate workers' compensation claims filed with state Department of Labor and Employment Security offices in Gainesville and Jacksonville.

The three men — Jesse Nash of Lake City, Gary Pittman of Jennings and Clinton Vann of Live Oak

— say exposure to chemicals used to manufacture phosphoric and and other products at the White Springs plant is to blame for a variety of illnesses and their inability to continue to work.

"I intend to fight these people down to the wire," Pittman said "And I'm not a fighter at heart, but now it's a mission."

Nash's claim is against both Occidental and PCS Phosphate, because he worked for both companies during his 18-year tenure in the plant's shipping department

PCS Phosphate bought Occidental's operation Oct 31 1995.

Please see CHEMICAL, 6B

12

Chapter One

When I first started working at the Occidental Chemical Corporation's phosphoric acid plants in the early 1970s, there was no safety program in place. The only safety equipment we were required to wear were hardhats and safety glasses. They never enforced wearing of the safety glasses. The environment was very dirty and the air was filled with dust and toxic fumes. We worked eight to twelve hours day, sometimes even longer in those conditions.

Most of the union work force was uneducated. Some graduated from high school and some could only barely read and write.

Occidental trained us, and most of us became skilled at our trades. However, my coworkers and I had no idea about the dangers to our health from working in that environment.

At 18-20 years old and you think you will live forever. Old age is never coming. Mistakenly, you tend to believe that you're somehow invincible and blindly step into harm's way without a thought about the future consequences.

I got married about that time, and my only worry was about making money and securing a comfortable life for my family and me. But there comes a time when you realize that you're just a frail human, and ask yourself if the good pay and job security was worth the price now being paid by you and your family.

I woke up this morning sometime around four-thirty with a dull pain in my hips and lower back. As the intensity of the pain increased, getting back to sleep was out of the question; so I headed off to the bathroom and splashed some cold water on my face. Staring into my reflection in the mirror, I knew all too well what the rest of morning held in store for me.

It was all so predictable. After the first jolt of throbbing pain, I managed, as usual, to gain my composure and hobble off to the kitchen where I kept my medications.

Just last week on a visit to Georgia, I ended up in the emergency room with serious heart arrhythmias; so first off, I popped one pill for the heart arrhythmias, then one pill to ease the inflammation in my hips, and a painkiller for fast pain relief.

Sitting at the kitchen table in the predawn hours, I thought about my last visit to the doctor when he said, "Gary, you can't take this kind of pain for too long." Then he said that I needed to have both hips replaced – an eventuality that I'm putting off for as long as possible.

Well, the next pill in the box was my Prozac – that's been a needed companion for many years now that I would rather live without. I suffer with bouts of depression due to long-term deteriorating health problems related to chemical exposures when I worked in the phosphate fertilizer industry.

I just went to my psychiatrist yesterday with a troubling outcome. I've experienced progressive memory loss for years and more recently, hallucinations during the night. Now the hallucinations are starting to get frightening like seeing bizarre scenes that are real to me and difficult to describe to anyone else.

At the end of the last session, my psychiatrist diagnosed me with early stages of presenile dementia and prescribed a medication to try to slow the progression of the disease.

It was in 1993, after a career spanning twenty-one years in the phosphate Industry, the day-in day-out exposures to chemicals and toxic vapors caught up with me. I came home from work early sick as a dog, vomiting, and I had an unbearable headache. Later that night, I was coughing up blood. At first, I thought it was a virus, but no one else in the house had any symptoms, but it was the beginning of a downward spiral as far as my health was concerned.

Back in 1996, I had a *Brain Spect*[2] Scan (imaging process) at a specialty clinic in Texas. They found exposure to the brain from the fumes and chemicals in my work environment, and said my condition would only get worse as time went on. They called it "Toxic Brain Syndrome."

---

* **SPECT Scan**: a type of nuclear imaging test, which means it uses a radioactive substance and a special camera to create 3-D pictures. SPECT scans produce 1mages that show how the organs work. For instance, a SPECT scan can show how blood flows to your heart or what areas of your brain are more active or less active.

My first and last job was working for the Occidental Chemical Corporation's phosphoric acid plants in Hamilton County, Florida.

I was 18 and in excellent health when I started work as a sample man in the analytical laboratory of the corporation's Suwannee River Plant. I rose to supervise one-third of Occidental's Swift Creek plant, earning about $50,000 a year. However, my success came at a high price – my health and wellbeing.

Now, seeing the handwriting on the wall, I decided it is time to tell the story about my career and experiences in the Phosphate Industry before it's too late so others can benefit from my experiences.

Hamilton County, Florida – The Setting

In the mid-1960s, they constructed Interstate 75 just south of Jennings, Florida. This made the old tourist trail, Highway 41, obsolete except for local traffic. Consequently, the tourism traffic through Jennings died, and the businesses and jobs disappeared.

Upon entering Jennings, a sign reads home of Andrew Prine. Andrew Prine is an accomplished actor who starred in Broadway plays, Hollywood movies, and television shows. He lives in Beverly Hills, California and is one of Hamilton County's favorite sons.

Jasper is the county seat of Hamilton County, and also located on U.S. 41. That's where most of the Counties' business affairs take place. It has a courthouse, three banks, grocery stores and several small businesses. Jasper, like Jennings got hurt economically by the Interstate 75 bypass.

White Springs on the southern end of the county is most famous for the Steven Foster Memorial Park located in the center of town.

The major employers in Hamilton County are PCS Phosphate and Florida Department of Corrections. There are also many small businesses employing people as well as the County.

PCS Phosphate is a Canadian based fertilizer company (Potash Corporation of Saskatchewan Inc). In 1995, PCS purchased the Florida based phosphate mines and processing facilities which were owned by Occidental Chemical Company, a subsidiary of Occidental Petroleum.

All in all, Hamilton County is still a beautiful part of Florida with an idyllic rural flavor and very little crime.

My Early Years

As for myself, I was born November 9th 1953 in Valdosta, Georgia about twenty miles north of Jennings, Florida. Little Griffin Hospital was the closest hospital to our home. Within a few days, my parents took me back to our small farm about four miles south of Jennings.

I was rarely sick during my early childhood and my mother took me to the pediatrician for regular check ups.

Our family made a modest living farming with my father also worked another job in town to make ends meet.

We didn't have everything we wanted but got what we needed.

Some of my first memories were working on the farm. Back in those days, the late 1950s, most of the work on small farms was done by using hand tools.

We grew Tobacco, corn, vegetables, and raised hogs. Farming in those days was hard work. We started early and worked late.

During the tobacco-harvesting season, the workday would start about four thirty in the morning and continue until about five or six in the evening.

I learned to work hard at an early age – everyone in the family had to chip-in to make ends meet and bring the crops in. That's just how it was on a small farm - a fact of life.

I started school in 1958 at Jennings. It was a country school where you started in grade one and graduated in grade twelve.

I made good grades and got along well with my classmates and teachers.

The county consolidated all the three schools in 1965, so I started 7th grade at the new Hamilton County High Complex.

Times were changing. Life was different at the new school. We had larger classrooms, more people, and things just didn't seem organized.

The country was also changing, and I could feel it even in my small rural town in North Florida.

The Vietnam War was heating up and many young men found themselves drafted into military service.

Then there was the Civil Rights issue. My school was slowly going through the process of integration with a small number of African American kids attending. I knew some of the black guys pretty well; we worked in the fields together.

There was a lot of tension during that period of my life caused by many changes going on in the country. Protests about the war, racial integration in the southern schools, the hippie culture, and changes in pop music all came into play to create an era of social upheaval and confusion for me.

All these influences hindered me from applying myself in high school like I should have. To a point, I got caught-up in the new movement, and basically, just coasted through high school.

I graduated in 1971 from Hamilton County High and took the summer off not knowing what I wanted to do with my future.

In the fall of 1971, I started attending the Orlando School of Computer Programming. Life was different for me there. The city was large compared to where I grew up, and I needed a job to pay rent, eat, and stay in school. I attended for about three months and was doing well, but couldn't find a job that would fit my schedule. Consequently, I left school and went home to find work.

Chapter Two

PHOSPHATE MINING

I returned home from my stint at school and talked to my father and two cousins about their jobs at Occidental Chemical outside of White Springs. My father had started work there in 1965 and also my two cousins.

Everyone in the area almost affectionately referred to Occidental as "Oxy" because when the tourism died, it essentially propped up the local economy and a means to escape from scratching the dirt for a living.

My father was working in the Stores Department, my cousin Charles was in the floatation plant, and Douglas was a mechanic in the Maintenance Department.

All three told me that the job was regular - 40 hours per week or more. They also told me that the wages were the highest in the area and they offered benefits such as health insurance and retirement, which were unheard of in rural areas unless you worked for the county or post office.

After I talked with everyone, I decided to give phosphate mining a try. I applied for a job at Occidental Chemical (Oxy) about December of 1971. The fellow who took my application was an old retired drill sergeant. He told me to get a haircut and he might hire me. I told him I would - that day.

As a teenager, I had odd jobs besides farm work such as pumping gasoline. But the pay was poor, and at the time, Oxy seemed like the ideal, lifelong job with a future and chance for advancement.

Time marched on, and as Christmas approached, I still didn't hear anything from Oxy. I started thinking about other options such as joining the Army, but several of my hometown friends and a family member were killed in Vietnam and joining didn't look too promising an option to me at the time.

I finally received a phone call around the 20th of January from human resources and they offered me a job in the analytical laboratory as a sample man.

A sample man was a person who went all over the mines and chemical plant picking up samples for analyses at the company laboratory.

I reported to human resources and was handed some papers to take to Lake City to see an Oxy doctor for a health physical. After arriving, the doctor checked my height, weight, blood pressure, had me perform several functions such as bending over, squatting and jumping jacks. The doctor signed off on the paperwork and wrote on the paper, "A perfect health specimen."

I took the paperwork back to human resources where they told me to report to the analytical laboratory at Suwannee River Chemical Complex at 0700 hours the next morning. The job was 40 hours per week - shift work, and the pay was $400 per month.

Florida Phosphate mining and processing started in the late 19th Century. They dubbed it, "Florida's Black Gold," and thousands of prospectors swarmed Florida in search of riches. It was like the California gold rush.

Phosphate mining in Florida began using picks, shovels, and wheelbarrows. Presently, they use mostly enormous electrically powered large draglines (strip mining) to mine hundreds of acres and millions of tons a year.

Dragline

Today, Florida mines produce over 75% of the United States and 25% of world's phosphate.

Processing phosphate rock is the separation from a mix of sand, clay, and phosphate that makes up the matrix layer. This matrix layer is anywhere between 15-50 feet below the earth's surface in Florida mines.

In Central Florida's 'Bone Valley' region, they mine about 1.3 million acres of land.

Next in the process, a machine called a ball mill receives raw phosphate rock and grinds it for use in the processing plants.

They separate the phosphate from the matrix by a process called froth floatation which occurs in a designated facility – called the float plant. The formal name for the process is "Beneficiation."

At the float plant, they pump the matrix containing phosphate into pneumatic cells (tanks) where they add a fatty acid (carboxylic acid like vinegar) and fuel oil (kerosene). Then with help from injected air bubbles, the phosphate rises to the top in a frothy mixture, which goes through a skimming process and further processing.

When I started work at the Suwannee River Chemical Complex on January 24th 1972 in the Analytical Laboratory as a sample man. I was eighteen years old and in excellent health.

My job was to drive from plant to plant, mining areas, float plants, washers, and to waste water canals or wherever we need samples taken at, and then we prepared them for chemical analysis.

The places where I took samples from were often miles apart.

Sometimes they pumped the raw slurry from strip mines several miles away to the beneficiation plant.

The preparation of samples required many different steps. We then mixed wet samples of phosphate rock, feed, product, and general tailings by hand, placed them in small pans, and baked until dry inside a large conventional oven.

Once dried, the samples were ground into a powder for chemical analysis. We also picked up samples of DAP (Di-ammonium Phosphate) and TSP (Tri-ammonium Phosphate) granulated fertilizers along with samples of sulfuric acid, phosphoric acid, and gypsum cake from the phosphoric acid plant.

I became very familiar with all the chemical plant and mining operations during that time.

The whole operation was very intimidating when I first started. There was a lot of noise, dust, caustic fumes, and hazards in the area. I had to get the hang of working in those chaotic, noisy, noxious environments. I also had to be very careful and look for leaks in the plants especially in the sulfuric and phosphoric acid areas.

They promoted me to a technician after about eight months. Then I began doing analysis on all samples from the chemical plant and mining operations.

There were four shifts of lab workers on a seven-day, rotating shift. A shift crew entailed one supervisor, four technicians, and a sample prep man. We analyzed control samples for the plants to stay on specifications, shipping samples to ensure quality, and prospect samples from the field to give the mining crew results on where and how deep to dig.

I gained a lot of knowledge working in the lab learning about the chemical properties of all aspects of the operation, where problem areas are, and how to keep track of all the wastewater and what is in it.

We could even take samples and find where leaks were occurring even if they were very small.

I worked about two years in the Analytical Laboratory and became interested in venturing into the plants.

I found the chemical plants intriguing and promotions were more numerous simply because the work force was larger and there was a greater turnover of personnel.

The Analytical Laboratory was a salaried position whereas the operators in the chemical plant were union. This created a problem when I wanted to enter the union workforce because I didn't have any department seniority. I had plant-wide seniority due to my company service, but that didn't count when it came to getting a good position in another area.

I talked to the chief chemist and manager about my proposed venture. I also talked with the president of the local union represented by International Chemical Workers Union Local 784, an affiliate of AFL/CIO. After much discussion, they allowed me to bid on a union job using my plant-wide seniority. I was the first employee to ever leave the Lab and enter the union workforce at this facility.

However, I was limited on what job I could win a bid on due to lack of department seniority. I had to start near the bottom and work my way up. I bid on a sizer operator job at the Suwannee River Mine at the floatation plant where the phosphate rock is separated from the clay and general tailings (sand).

That was the start down a new path, and I was gaining even more knowledge about the operations along the way.

It only took about two days for me to wish I were back in the lab. The sizer operator job was dirty, wet, and always hectic. My job was to control the raw feed bins from the pit where the dragline dug and pumped the slurried feed.

I also had to size the rock using screens. The raw feed came down through dewatering cyclones into the screens for sizing. Lines would plug, screens would fall in the chutes, and it was just problem after problem - all shift long. That's when I realized why I was the successful bidder for that job; no one else wanted it.

I came in to work one day at 0700 hours and at 1500 hours after my shift, I had no relief, he was a no show. I had to work another shift until 2300 hours and then there was another no show. I already worked 16 hours and had to work on. After a 24-hour shift, I finally got off and went home for a well-needed rest.

I had walked through that plant in a pair of wet rubber boots for 24 straight hours and when I got home had water blisters the size of nickels on both feet. I had to stay out of work for two days and needed two additional days off to recoup.

I worked at the beneficiation plant for several more months as an assistant floatation operator. I learned how to float rock (separate phosphate rock from clay and sand). When I got the chance to get out, I did!

The float crews didn't get any special protective gear like clothes, dust masks, or respirators.

Around the chemical plant and washer, the wastewater was a mix of all the phosphoric acid processing wastes, mud, and whatever toxic wastes they wanted to get rid of. When things went wrong, we had to slosh into it.

Sometimes, we would be up to our waists in it for the whole shift. It smelled of chemicals and stagnant water - a stinking blue-grey slime with an oily slick floating on top of it.

I remember going into the Suwannee River complex and seeing catfish lying belly-up in the ditches with blisters on their bellies and backs. We hardly ever saw any birds or animals around the ponds.

Occasionally, animals would drink at one of the evaporation ponds, and not long after, I'd see them lying dead – even the damn flies and buzzards knew better than to snatch an easy meal off the toxic carcasses laying out there on the open embankments.

Nothing much lived around those ponds. The trees and plants were all burnt and dead from the acid fumes. It looked like what you'd imagine as the aftermath of an atomic war.

It was approaching winter, and I was looking for a warm place to work, so I placed a bid for 'issue clerk' at the Stores Department and won it.

'Stores' was a huge warehouse where they kept all the spare parts and supplies for the entire operation. I worked there through the winter of 1974 building more seniority.

My job was to put up stock and issue parts and supplies as Oxy required. I held this position for about three months. In the spring of 1975, I bid on an evaporator operator job in the old Dorr Oliver Phosphoric Acid Plant and won the bid.

Chapter Three

I received a phone call in April 1975, and the plant manager was on the other end. He knew me from my lab days and told me I won the evaporator operator position at Dorr Oliver and he wanted me to take it.

I was leery about taking the job because it was near the top of the pay scale, and I wondered why not anyone with any seniority in the department didn't already snap the job up.

I was damn sure I didn't want another job from hell like the sizer-operator at the floatation plant. I still cringe at the thought of the sizer-operator job. If anything went wrong, I had to wade waste deep in the slimy mess and fix things. It was hot and nasty during the summer, and cold and miserable during the winter. It was probably the worst job in the whole company.

Thinking that I might be jumping out of the frying pan into the fire, I asked my old supervisor, straight up, why no one bid on the job. He said that there had been some modifications to the evaporators and they were kicking everyone's ass. He said that he recommended me because he thought I was a good troubleshooter and could handle the job.

He knew me pretty well as we had worked some together on projects through the Analytical Lab. He assured me that I would have no problem with the job, and that I would get two weeks training. Still somewhat leery, I accepted the position.

What I didn't know at the time was that I would spend the next eighteen-years working in Phosphoric Acid related plants for Occidental Chemical.

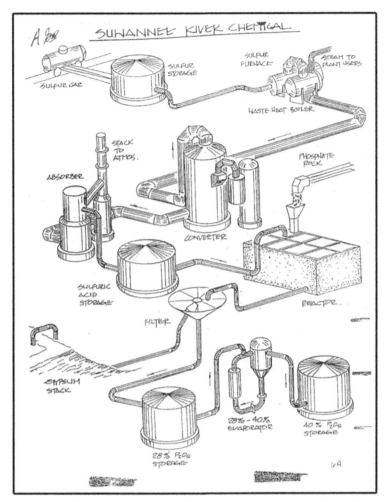

The figure is a hand-drawn diagram titled "SUWANNEE RIVER CHEMICAL" showing labeled equipment: SULFUR CAR, SULFUR STORAGE, SULFUR FURNACE, STEAM TO PLANT USERS, WASTE HEAT BOILER, STACK TO ATMOS., ABSORBER, CONVERTER, PHOSPHATE ROCK, SULFURIC ACID STORAGE, FILTER, REACTOR, GYPSUM STACK, 28% P₂O₅ STORAGE, 28%-40% EVAPORATOR, 40% P₂O₅ STORAGE.

In the spring of 1975, I started work in the old Dorr-Oliver Phosphoric Acid plant at Suwannee River Chemical Complex.

Occidental constructed the Dorr-Oliver plant in 1967, and it came on-line in 1968.

They named the plant Dorr-Oliver for the process used to produce phosphoric acid. There are many processes used today to produce phosphoric acid.

We used a "wet/acidulation process" to produce phosphoric acid. It was the addition of the raw phosphate rock slurry to a mixture of concentrated sulfuric acid and evaporation pond water in a large reactor vessel. There, we continuously mixed it with agitators that looked like giant blending machines so the sulfuric acid could digest (dissolve) the phosphate rock. That process produced a slurry which needed to go through a filtration process to separate the solids from the phosphoric acid.

When sulfuric acid reacts with the phosphate rock, it causes what they call an exothermic reaction – meaning that it produces a great deal of heat. We used a concentrated sulfuric acid solution so the reaction was even more intense.

The acidulation also caused a lot of foaming and released a large volume of noxious, toxic fumes.

The foaming was so bad, we had to use a defoamer which is an oil based liquid that control the foaming to keep the mixture from bubbling over the top of the reactor vessels like a washing machine that when someone added too much soap powder.

When the reaction process was finished, the mixture looked like a mud pie. Then we'd pump the slurry into a large rotating filter which had twenty-four pans.

Next, huge vacuum pumps under the filter dewatered the slurry, and deposited the liquid phosphoric acid in the filtration tank. Then we pumped the filtered acid into a product tank. The leftover phosphoric acid, we either recycled the back to the reactor vessel or used to 'weak-wash' (clean) the filter.

There was a vacuum cooler to maintain the heat in the reactor at 170-180 degrees Fahrenheit, otherwise things could have really got nasty. If the exothermic reaction form mixing the concentrated sulfuric acid with the slurry wasn't controlled, the outcome would have been disastrous, caused a large release of toxic fumes, and caused serious injuries to the plant workers.

The process sucked slurry through a large pipe into a vessel where cold water travels through a condenser (pipes), cools the slurry, and deposits it back into the reactor thus keeping a constant temperature. Essentially, the cooling process is like how a kitchen refrigerator or an air conditioner works.

The fumes from the process are extremely toxic and corrosive which is damaging to the lungs and health in general.

They contain hydrogen fluoride, and silicon tetrafluoride, which are the two most corrosive substances know. Then there were a host of nasty, carcinogenic radioactive substances like radium, polonium, and radon – then add some hydrogen sulfide and sulfur dioxide along with a few other processing chemicals to that toxic concoction and you've got some really nasty, corrosive toxic mix.

One of the main reasons for processing the raw phosphate rock for agricultural purposes is because of the fluoride content – mainly in the form of fluorosilicates/silicon tetrafluoride.

Back in the early part of the 20th century when industrial farming was first starting-up, they did many experiments on cheap mineral supplements for animals to keep costs down and profits up.

Raw, powdered phosphate rock was the first choice because of the abundance and it was dirt-cheap. Bone meal was the second choice, but it was more expensive because it had needed cooking in ovens (calcining) at high temperatures before the animals could digest it properly.

When the animal nutrition researchers did the first experiments with the powdered phosphate rock, the animals started to get sick. The cow's milk was drying-up, and there was a high rate of calf stillbirths.

It was really knocking the pigs' health for a loop – many of them became so sick, they just quit eating, quit breeding, and the researchers said they seemed to give up the will to live.

Well, as for the chickens, they just up and died after eating food supplemented with the raw phosphate rock.

They knew that fluorides were toxic and determined that it was the fluorides, but in later experiments, they found that it wasn't just any type of fluoride, but the fluorosilicates that were doing most of the damage.

They used sodium fluoride (like what they use in toothpaste) and sodium fluorosilicate to compare the poisonous effects on the farm animals, and found that the sodium fluorosilicate was a much more effective poison.

Another reason for processing the raw phosphate rock is that the fluoride content is also enough to be toxic to many agricultural crops – the raw rock will actually inhibit the growth of crops. Some plants like gladiolas will just wilt will die when fertilized with raw phosphate rock because of the fluoride content.

The outcome of those early studies strongly suggested that using raw phosphate rock as a cheap fertilizer or animal mineral supplement the way to go if you wanted to make a profit and have healthy plants and animals.

Because of occupational safety and environmental protection laws, there are fume ducts and fume (pollution) scrubbers on the reactor, filter feed tank, and above the filter that lead to the fume scrubber that are required. These harmful fumes must go through the fume scrubber before discharged into the atmosphere through a smokestack.

In simple terms, a fume (pollution) scrubber works on the same principle of how rain cleans dust out of the air.

When the phosphoric acid leaves the filtering stage, it's about 28% phosphoric acid, and then it must be concentrated further before it goes for further processing in other parts of the chemical plant or sold as a merchant grade acid.

Essentially, the phosphoric acid is the plant food part of fertilizer.

My new job was an Evaporator Operator. My task was to take the 28% phosphoric acid and make it stronger.

Looking back, there's only one-way to describe the Dorr-Oliver plant; it was about the roughest looking, scariest places I'd ever seen during the day, but at night, it was particularly frightening - like what you would imagine that Hell looked like.

Choking, eye burning, noxious fumes permeated the air and steam was billowing out everywhere. The noise was deafening as the motors and pumps ran simultaneously. A lot of the pumps were belt-driven, especially the vacuum pumps.

When the pumps were pushing a heavy load, the belts slipped and make an ear-piercing squeal that could send chills up Satan's spine.

Hot phosphoric acid dripped here and there leaving puddles on the floor. Regular leather work-boots didn't stand a chance in hell against the acid. If you were exceptionally careful where you stepped, leather boots would still only last two or three weeks – that is, if you were lucky.

I learned damned quick that a man would be wise to invest in a pair of acid resistant rubber boots.

The evaporators consisted of three large vessels each with carbon tube heat exchangers and circulating pumps that circulated the acid through the heat exchangers. The heat exchangers used low-pressure steam generated by the sulfuric acid plants to evaporate the water from the phosphoric acid.

The three evaporators ran in series, A, B, and C. We pumped 28% feed acid from a storage tank to the evaporators A, B, and C cooking and evaporating in each stage until you reached the strength you wanted.

We made two strengths at the time. The 40% concentration acid went to the granulation plant to manufacture granulated fertilizer. The defluorinated 50% concentration went to polyphosphoric to make animal feed supplement or sold as a finished product.

The Dorr-Oliver phosphoric acid plant operated twenty-four hours a day seven days a week. We only shut down for repair days and turnaround. Repair days occurred about every two weeks and took about twelve hours to complete.

Most maintenance was done while we were still operating by switching to the spare pumps.

Turnarounds were major repairs and cleaning performed by shutting down for about a week then draining and washing all vessels.

It required four shifts to operate the plant. A shift consisted of a Shift Supervisor, Operator A, Evaporator Operator, Operator B, Operator C, and a Helper.

Operator A controlled the reaction side of the plant with help from the B and C. Mainly working alone, the evaporator operator controlled the evaporation side of the plant.

The helper floated around the plant and assisted everyone as needed.

The Shift Supervisor supervised the whole crew and gave orders daily as Oxychem dictated.

After about a year, I became comfortable with my job and the hellish atmosphere at Suwannee River Chemical Complex. By then, I had about four years experience at Oxychem and had a working knowledge about how everything fit together.

In 1975, the chemical facility was like a small town with each plant and employees doing their jobs to make overall operation run as smoothly as possible.

Suwannee River Chemical Complex consisted of two Sulfuric Acid plants. Solid raw sulfur came to the plant by rail in special tank cars that have steam coils inside. Once the tank cars are in place, steam hoses they attached to the coils on the tank cars, then the solid sulfur is heated with low-pressure steam (about 335 degrees Fahrenheit) from a boiler until the solid sulfur is molten - usually red hot. We then produced sulfuric acid from the molten sulfur.

Sulfuric acid is the main ingredient used to produce phosphoric acid. Occidental also sold some to other industries.

We also produced Granulated fertilizer at the complex. The Granulation plant consisted of two plants or trains, X and Y train.

To produce the granulated fertilizer is a process where they mix ground phosphate rock, phosphoric acid and other ingredients such as nitrates and mineral combinations depending on the agricultural uses.

Next is the polyphosphoric, which is an animal feed supplement to make the animals bones hard, chicken eggshells hard, and to supply other essential minerals.

The polyphosphoric plant made the animal feed supplement. The process to make polyphosphoric is essentially mixing phosphoric acid with phosphate rock and adding caustic soda (sodium hydroxide) together. Then it goes through a cooking process in reactors to drive off as much of the fluorine (fluorides) as possible from the phosphate rock and phosphoric acid.

The reason for driving off the fluorine (fluorides) is that it is toxic to farm animals, and especially to pigs and chickens.

The US Department of Agricultural regulations for fluoride levels in animal feedstock and mineral supplements are more stringent than the Federal Food and Drug administration allows for humans.

All in all, producing phosphoric acid business is a dirty complex business, but for better or worse, it is a fact of modern life.

Chapter Four

There were about 400-500 people working at Oxy in 1975 including the support groups.

It was a large operation putting out large volumes of phosphoric acid on a daily basis and generating huge volumes of toxic wastes in the process.

Gypsum is the main byproduct in the waste stream of phosphoric acid production. When they filter the phosphoric acid from the slurry, gypsum is left. Then the phosphoric acid plant reslurries the gypsum and pumps it to an evaporation pond where it's removed and stacked around the perimeter forming a dam. The pile of waste gypsum just gets higher and higher and higher as the years goes on.

If you drive past a phosphate mine or chemical plant, you will see mountains of these phosphogypsum stacks. So, along with the general toxic emissions from processing phosphoric acid, the evaporation ponds also give off toxic, fluoride emissions into the atmosphere.

The EPA is always trying to help industry to find markets for industrial waste products like phosphogypsum. One way they found to get rid of it and turn it into a profit source for the industry was to sell it to farmers. It's supposed to be a good source of calcium and sulfur for the soil. The farmers just spread it on top of the soil, but if they use it to control the acidity and alkalinity of the soil, they till it into the ground.

US farmers use about 221,000 metric tons of phosphogypsum a year. There're no limitations on how much they can use, and the farmers don't have to have certificates or application records.

The gypsum stacks and ponds where they dump the waste cover more than 100,000 acres in Florida's mining regions. It can take three to five years for a full settling into a useable landform.

The waste gypsum also contains trace metals in concentrations that the EPA believes may pose a threat to human health and the environment. The analysis of samples taken from various facilities contained arsenic, lead, cadmium, chromium, fluoride, zinc, antimony, and copper at concentrations that may pose significant health risks.

The radium wastes from filtration systems at phosphate fertilizer facilities are among the most radioactive types of naturally occurring radioactive material (NORM) wastes. They can only be disposed of at the one US landfill licensed to accept NORM wastes in Nevada.

Consequently, the manufacturers just dump the radioactive wastes in acidic ponds atop 200-foot-high gypsum stacks rather than go to the expense of shipping it off across the country. The federal government has no rules for its disposal.

The concentrations of uranium and radium in waste gypsum are about 10 times the background levels in soil for uranium and 60 times the background levels in soil for radium.

They tried using the phosphogypsum in a Portland cement mixture for road construction. However, in 1992, the EPA banned it's use because it was too radioactive.

Another interesting fact:

Florida phosphate rock has high concentrations of uranium-238 and produced most of the uranium used to make the first atomic bombs. Today, the US phosphate industry produces more yellow cake uranium then uranium mines for the nuclear power industry.

Back to the story: At the time, back in 1975, OSHA (Occupational Safety and Health Administration) regularly fined Occidental for safety violations[3].

About that time, there was also a big stink about emissions from the granulation plants where they make the dry phosphate fertilizer. The FDEP (Florida Department of Environmental Protection) found wrongdoing about emissions and said heads were about to roll. But I don't recall anything ever coming of it. At a much later date, I discovered it was just so much hot wind, because beside the citrus industry, the phosphate industry rules the roost in Florida.

On repair days and turnarounds, we would have to go inside these vessels to clean them and clean the pollution scrubbers. There was always residue and phosphoric acid left over inside the vessels and fluorosilicate dust in the scrubbers. Buildup would form inside on the walls and floors from months of operating. This buildup was like a semi hard concrete. We had to use chipping hammers to break it away and haul out the material with wheel barrels.

---

* See Appendix: Occidental OSHA safety violation from 1973-1991.

I remember one time when they assigned me the task of cleaning the filter hood on the pollution scrubber. Powdery fluorosilicate dust was everywhere. As we were cleaning, the dust covered us. It was very hot - 100 to 120 degrees - and we were sweating profusely. When the fluorosilicate dust mixed with the perspiration, it formed acid on the skin and blistered us if we didn't wash it off in time. We were breathing those dusts, too. They didn't give us respirators.

Driving home after that episode cleaning a pollution scrubber, I was coughing and choking. My eyes started to burn and I realized that my clothes were fuming. The fumes got so thick that I had to roll the window down in my truck so I could see to drive. When I got home, I removed my clothes and gave them to my wife to wash. Well, the only things that came out of the washing machine intact were the zipper and buttons attached to numerous frayed rags.

I also remember a woman who worked at Oxy in the accounting department telling me about when they went to work and got out of their cars in the morning, their panty hose would dissolve off their legs and their cars got acid etched. The management told them not to not to worry; it was just harmless chemical fallout and gave them a weekly allowance to buy new panty hose.

Once inside those vessels and scrubbers, we had no respirators, and had to breathe that stale, moist acidic air all shift. Sometimes, workers would fall ill with flu-like symptoms, the older works called it "chemical pneumonia."

During my career, I experienced chemical pneumonia many times.

When we had to clean the pollution scrubbers, most of us went home with acid burns and coughing up blood.

The drinking water at the plant came from nearby wells.

I suspected that wastewater from the holding ponds were leaching into the aquifer that supplied Oxy's drinking water. When the lab tested the water, they found the fluoride levels were 15 to 17 parts per million - four times the EPA's MCL (Maximum Contaminant Level) for drinking water.

The phosphoric acid levels in the water were also very high.

The drinking water was so laden with corrosive chemicals that the metal pipes carrying it crumbled.

Eventually, the drinking water became so contaminated that the employees complained that it was undrinkable. Oxy installed a reverse osmosis system, but contaminants soon clogged the system and rendered it ineffective. After that, most everybody brought their own water, or drank soft drinks to work.

Just from working at the facilities, everyday workers got a daily dose of fluorides, dusts, radiation, and much more for years and years. The management didn't have regular testing of the workforce to monitor the exposures to the dangerous substances in that environment.

Generally, most companies do regular urine test for chemical exposures to avoid potential litigation.

In 1976, phase two began at Suwannee River Chemical Complex. Armand Hammer the driving behind Occidental Petroleum, our parent company, negotiated a barter agreement with the Soviet Union.

Armand Hammer was an American industrialist best known for his close relationship with the Occidental, which he ran for decades and his controversial ties with Soviet Union leaders, Vladimir Lenin and Josef Stalin. He was also close friends with President Ronald Regan.

Occidental Chemical at White Springs would produce Super Phosphoric Acid and deliver it to Russia in exchange for urea that is loaded with nitrogen.

This large undertaking would require major expansion of the facilities at White Springs. Oxy started building new sulfuric acid and phosphoric acid plants to meet production demands for the Soviet Union project.

About this time, management decided to shut down the old plants due to slow sales. The warehouses were full of product, and they made the decision to perform a major turnaround on the existing plants during this slow time. These slow-downs happen from time to time and it affects the whole industry.

Oxy contracted Davy-Powergas and Chemical Tolling Company to build the new plants needed for the Soviet Union Super Acid Project production. A lot of building and repairing went on at the plants.

The old Dorr-Oliver phosphoric acid plant where I worked was shutdown for repairs.

Previously, Oxy built a small pilot plant for testing in anticipation of the Super Acid deal with the Soviet Union.

After months of research, the Research and Development Department found that in order to keep Super Phosphoric Acid liquefied in the huge tankers on their journey from Florida to the Soviet Union, we would somehow have to remove some elemental metals from the acid.

Super Phosphoric Acid (SPA) is very thick like honey and in that form would tend to set up or crystallize on the long trip.

The new pilot plant named Solvent Extraction was designed to remove some of these elements from the SPA. I was one of the original A

Operators of the Solvent Extraction Plant. My work in the analytical laboratory years earlier helped me a lot in this plant.

The plant was easy for me to understand and operate. Our main goal was to remove magnesium from the phosphoric acid. The plant consisted of a group of separate cells that allowed phosphoric acid to be pumped in on one end and move through each cell until it came out the other end.

We started by pumping Dinonylnaphthalene Sulfonic acid (DNSA) into the cells along with kerosene. The usual reaction solvents were benzene, hexane, and heptanes. The fumes in the plant were very strong and made you dizzy. If you didn't get to some fresh air once in a while, you could find yourself unconscious down on the floor.

We would then pump in the phosphoric acid at a given rate along with a small amount of sulfuric acid. The magnesium, some aluminum, and iron would attach to the DNSA and the phosphoric acid would come out the other end with less metals. We operated this plant for about three months.

When they repaired the Dorr-Oliver plant and it was operational, we brought the plant back online.

The new sulfuric and phosphoric acid plants were almost complete, and I wanted to work in the new plants so I planned to bid for a job there as soon as they were complete.

The new phosphoric acid plant would actually be two plants in one. One was a 1000 ton per day Prayon process. The other plant was a small 350 ton per day experimental Oxy process. When the plants were finished in 1976-77, I was an operator of the new Oxy Hemihydrate process.

The Hemihydrate process was different from Dorr-Oliver or Prayon in that the Oxy process would produce 40% acid right off the filter where Dorr-Oliver and Prayon only produced 28%. The Hemihydrate process would save money by dropping an evaporation stage.

We finally perfected the new Oxy process after much hard work and trial and error.

Oxy was building a new mining operation near Jasper and planning on building a 1200-ton per day Oxy Hemihydrate Phosphoric acid Plant. This plant would be the flagship for the Soviet Union Agreement and would produce the phosphoric acid we needed.

In 1978 after the successful start up of the Oxy Hemihydrate Process, they offered me a shift Supervisor position supervising both the Prayon and Oxychem phosphoric acid plants at Suwannee River Chemical Complex.

At one time, I supervised Dorr-Oliver too.

I was 25 years old at the time. I took the job because it was a salaried position with good pay, benefits, and I really liked my manager. I worked in this position until the fall of 1979 when Oxy finished building the giant Hemihydrate Phosphoric Acid Plant at the new Swift Creek Mine and Chemical Complex.

In the fall of 1979, we started up the new Hemi phosphoric acid plant at Swift Creek.

Everything was very large. It was like the Goliath of phosphoric acid plants. Vessels were huge, the pumps were monsters, and the filter was the largest of its kind in the world. We got the plant online and produced tons and tons of acid over the years.

I left Oxy for a short time in 1980 to run the family farm. I was just plain tired, burnt out, and needed a break.

I returned to Oxy in 1985 as a Shipping Supervisor in charge of shipping and receiving of raw materials. We shipped out Super Phosphoric Acid, sulfuric acid, and merchant grade phosphoric acid and received sulfur, ground limestone, fuel oils, and defoamers.

I didn't like shipping at all. It was boring to me because I was used to working in the plants producing product. I also hated the sulfur unloading station. The fumes from the molten sulfur give me to most awful headaches.

I worked at shipping about three months and transferred to Evaporation/Purification.

Evaporation/Purification included three low-pressure evaporators, two high-pressure evaporators or SPA's where we produced Super Phosphoric Acid. It also contained a synspar plant (synthetic fluorspar) from the scrubber liouor.

Last, was the Filter building where phosphoric acid was purified before feeding it to the SPA's for the production of Super Phosphoric Acid. The end-result of the Filter Process produced the same as the Solvent Extraction process.

The plan was to evaporate the phosphoric acid and remove the elements (mainly magnesium and aluminum) then evaporate the phosphoric acid into Super Acid or 70%. I worked in E/P until May of 1993 producing Super Phosphoric Acid, mainly for the Occidental Chemical/Soviet Union Barter agreement.

Chapter Five

I began to have health problems as early as 1986.

In September 1986, a rash covered my arms, hands, and back. It was a round circular rash that started out small and grew leaving my skin white and scaly.

The rash was eating me alive.

My neighbor was a doctor, and I asked him to look at it. He said he had never saw anything like it before, but it might be a reaction to something or be mycotic, a disease caused by a fungus. He prescribed some cream and antibiotics and it finally cleared. I missed a couple days work because of it.

A few years later, my right hand started to swell and became painful.

When I went to the doctor, he told me I had a hairline fracture of the pinky finger. I didn't recall any injury to the finger and wondered how this could be.

As I continued to work in E/P, I experienced frequent colds, muscle weakness, joint pain, neck pain, dizziness, headaches, heart arrhythmias, and shortness of breath.

I seemed to stay sick all the time.

We worked in caustic fumes pouring off the hot acids, and so many of us developed respiratory infections, we thought it was caused by a virus in the air. We went around the plant armed with cans of disinfectant and sprayed telephones, walls, and air-conditioning ducts.

I developed serious ear infections, near constant upper respiratory tract infection and sebaceous cysts that I had to have removed from my hand.

In 1991, I got a promotion to Assistant Superintendent of E/P in charge of day-to-day operations and maintenance. This was about the time we had to start providing Material Safety Data Sheets to any worker that requested one for any chemical used in the plant.

The new occupational safety and health law gave us a window of time to get the job accomplished, and I had Oxy chemist providing me with our chemical MSDS sheets. I also started requesting MSDS sheets for chemicals we use from outside vendors.

The MSDS information for flocculants, solvents, defoamers, etc. started coming in, and I began compiling them into a large notebook in alphabetical order for anyone that wanted to view them.

I took the time to start reviewing each one to make sure we were providing proper safety equipment. I was surprised at the adverse effects these chemicals could have on a person's health.

At that time, I was working with a few specialty chemicals trying to improve some problems we had with in the process such as scale inhibitors, and slurry flocculants.

My health continued to deteriorate as time went on, but I hadn't put two and two together yet although I familiarized myself with the MSDS information.

We had two pollution scrubbers A and B. Management decided to shut one of the scrubbers down in the plant a couple of years before and the fumes were worse than normal. They were extremely bad when both scrubbers were running, but with one shut down the fumes were much worse.

The management told me that we did not need scrubber A, and scrubber B was sufficient. However, at the time, it surprised me because our operating permits from the state required that all the scrubbers needed to be operational during production and well maintained. I knew this was wrong but reporting this would have meant the loss of my job.

Looking back, I wish I had reported it. Scrubber A was supposed to scrub some of the more toxic fumes such as the fumes from the Super Phosphoric Acid evaporators.

Hydrogen fluoride and silicon tetrafluoride were the primary pollutants of concern from the operations. The USEPA has very stringent regulations about fluoride emissions because it's some pretty nasty stuff – it kills plants, and poisons people, fish, and animals.

Occidental routinely cheated on cooling stack emission tests because OSHA (Occupational Safety and Health Administration) and FDEP were required to give Oxy notice of inspections.

As far as inspections went, they were a joke.

OSHA or the FDEP always gave Oxy at least a few weeks notice before they came to do inspections. It was common practice to clean the pollution scrubbers when notified of an inspection.

When the FDEP were coming to visit the facility and do cooling stack tests for pollution emissions, Oxy management ordered a crew of mechanics to remove the spray bars and drag them out onto the street. We had to beat the pipes with nine-pound sledgehammers to break the solids loose.

It was also common practice to pull the scrubber pads onto the street and drive trucks over them to break the solidified fluorosilicates loose.

The nozzles were all plugged-up, and we had to try to clean them or if they were too bad, we just replaced them. Nothing could have passed through the nozzles, but somehow, we managed to get the pollution scrubber operational by the time inspectors showed up.

Management also had us open a blind on the fume duct to allow more fresh air into the fume stream so it would be dilute the emissions and pass the stack test (cheating).

When the FDEP or OSHA inspectors ran a test for cooling stack emissions, the test always came out looking good. I don't think the inspectors ever knew that Occidental was cheating on those tests - or they just didn't care. The FDEP and EPA allowed Occidental to be self-policing.

Back in the plant, the fumes in the SPA area were so bad that we couldn't breathe at the hot-wells. Some of the electricians complained so much that Oxy tested around this area. They said the fluoride levels were acceptable.

I smelled a rat and knew these fumes were not just fluoride. To me they were more like sulfur dioxide because you can't really smell the gaseous fluorides, but the sulfur vapors have a distinct rotten egg or burnt matches odor about them.

Our plant didn't have a permit for sulfur dioxide and of course, there were no test done for those.

Later, I had a chemical engineer calculate some numbers for me. He calculated the tons of sulfuric acid feed and the tons of product with the amount of sulfuric going in and out – essentially, the calculations were to determine how much stayed in the product and how much went into the atmosphere as a gas.

When he completed the calculations, it turned out our sulfur dioxide emissions were 2,123 tons a year or 4,246,663 pounds per year and our permit was 0.0 pounds.[4]

---

* See Appendix: Sulphuric Acid Emissions.

As far as the sulfur dioxide/hydrogen sulfide, a coworker who worked at the sulfuric acid plant told me that one day when they were down for maintenance, they blew the stacks (that's what the call cleaning them) and as the emissions went up into the atmosphere, a flock of birds were flying over. He said when they flew into the pollution; they just fell out of the sky like rocks - dead.

Sometimes, the concentrated airborne acidic cocktails at the Occidental plants would eat the paint off cars and etch windshields.

Secretaries sent to the plant on errands complained that their pantyhose were dissolving on their legs. The plant managers said it was nothing to be concerned about it was just harmless fumes!

Running pollution scrubbers is an expensive proposition – they need regular maintenance, they take electricity, and like most other industrial equipment, they need replacement once in awhile.

Some companies pump the recovered pollution which is fluorosilicic acid into tanks and sell it to fluoridate drinking water and other industries, but it's mainly used for fluoridating the drinking water to supposedly reduce tooth decay.

The point is that both the EPA and State environmental agencies allow phosphate companies and others to police themselves and money wins every time. I would bet that they are still emitting this sulfur dioxide as we speak, and the state either doesn't know or doesn't care.

However, one time, the Florida Department of Environmental Protection (FDEP) fined Oxy for releasing ten times the permitted levels of fluorides into the air, but that was a rare exception to the general rules of the game.

Chapter Six

In the fall of 1992, Oxy started downsizing the operation. The Soviet Union was no more and we lost our contract trading SPA for urea.

They transferred my boss to another area of the operation and I got a promotion to Area Supervisor, which meant that I did my job and his for the same money.

Competition for quality was fierce, and we had to start making our product better to compete with other phosphate companies in the USA.

In March 1993, I walked out of my office over to the main pipe rack to look at a product line, which was dripping and needed repair. When I finished inspecting the pipes and I started back to my office, my legs wouldn't move. I had feeling in both legs, but couldn't move them.

A couple of my operators were nearby, and I yelled to them to come and give me a hand. I placed each arm around each operator and managed to get back to my office where I sat down. After about an hour, I could finally move my legs, but they were still weak. By the time my shift over, I managed to hobble out to my car and drive home.

The next day my legs felt OK, but they were still a little weak. After that, as time went on, it seemed as if I was getting weaker and more fatigued. I got to the point where I couldn't walk up the stairs at the plant without resting.

I managed to work until May 1993 when my feet became so swollen, I could barely hobble around. I was having dizzy spells, episodes of confusion, and heart arrhythmias. All muscles in my body were weak and aching.

My benefits with Oxy included short and long-term disability insurance. On May 21, 1993, I had to leave work and start short-term disability. I was no longer able to do my job after twenty-one years of service.

I made an appointment with Dr. Leon Smith in Valdosta, Georgia. He was located about twenty-five miles from my home. I really didn't have a doctor at the time, and until that time, I never really needed one.

A few days passed, and I went to see Dr. Smith. During my initial examination, he had an EKG performed and drew blood for analysis. The results of the EKG showed that I had a heart attack, but it was an old scar.

I returned home and waited for the result of my blood analysis.

In the meantime, Occidental called repeatedly asking when I thought I might return to work. I could only tell them I didn't know and would keep them informed. They were shorthanded at the plant and concerned about how to they were going to keep production going.

The downsizing left a void of experienced personnel in my area, and Oxy was starting to panic a little bit.

In a few days, I had a follow up appointment with Dr. Smith and the news wasn't good. He told me that I had a muscle destructive process happening. My CPK's[5] were over 5000 which are abnormal. CPK is a test used to measure protein in the blood. When there is muscle damage, the reading goes high.

Dr. Smith told me I needed a specialist and referred me to a doctor in Tifton, Georgia, a rheumatologist. Dr. Smith wrote a letter for me to give to my employer about my condition, and I took it to my boss at Oxy.

The doctor in Tifton was booked up and he couldn't see me for two months. I was worried and started looking for a rheumatologist in Florida. I asked around and some friends and extended family gave me the names of several doctors.

I decided to go with Dr. Longley in Gainesville, Florida. His credentials were very good, and he also taught at University of Florida. Dr. Smith sent my records ahead for Dr. Longley to review before my appointment.

In the meantime, I started to think about what could have caused all these problems. I was only thirty-nine years old and in excellent health up to that point.

The MSDS information kept running through my mind.

I knew that all of the symptoms that I was experiencing could be due to previous chemical exposures from what I read on the MSDS's, but at the time, I just wanted to get better and go back to work. I had a family to support and mortgage to pay, and like most other people, I figured the doctor would give me a few pills, and I would be right as rain.

_____

[5] The CPK blood test is a very useful tool for helping doctors to diagnose muscle damage from heart attack, stroke, and injury.

In a telephone conversation, the plant manager at Oxy told me that my position was safe and just to get well.

It took me twenty-one years of hard work and long hours to get where I was at Oxy. I was making about fifty thousand dollars a year with Oxy matching my retirement account dollar for dollar. I also had good health insurance. My schedule was Monday through Friday, eight hours a day with weekends off. For most of my career, I did shift work.

My appointment with Dr. Longley went well. He stated that I had polymyositis and that my muscles would never be the same. He said that after six months I might be able to return to work if things went well. He said that he wanted to perform a muscle biopsy to check the muscle.

After having my blood work done again, my CPK's were still high but came down some since the first test. He also stated that he had seen cases where the muscles became so weak that a person would need to have a machine breathe for them.

They performed the biopsy at North Florida Regional Hospital in Gainesville, Florida, and I returned home and waited for results.

Life at home was stressful. My wife Gloria and I had four children, Nichol 15, Scarlett 7, Brittany 4 and James was about 4 months. In 1989, we bought a nice home in Lake Park, Georgia at Francis Lake. The home was on number three fairway and in a nice community.

I was drawing short-term disability insurance and it only paid about eighty percent of my salary. This meant we had to tighten our belts to stay on our budget. I was also very weak, in pain most of the time, and wasn't particularly good company for my family.

I returned to Dr. Longley about a month later feeling a little better. He gave me some Depo-Medrol shots and it helped the inflammation in my feet and muscles. He told me the biopsy did not show a typical polymyositis. Polymyositis means inflammation of many muscles.

I thought I was getting better, and Dr. Longley, at that time, told me I had a non-specific Myopathy, which meant he didn't know what the muscle disease was. He also told me I had autoimmune disease. Dr. Longley wanted to see me again in three months so he could see how I was doing and wrote me a prescription for Vioxx.

A few months went by since I first became ill, and I started to get restless. I had never been this sick before and was not used to being cooped up in a house with nothing to do I guess you'd say I was going stir-crazy.

I always took a lot of pride in my home and grounds. I loved to do the gardening work myself, but now, I was paying a lawn service to cut my grass and keep up my yard.

Chapter Seven

An old friend that I worked with back in my days at the Analytical Laboratory in the 1970s left work a few months before me. Clinton Vann and I were good friends back in those days, but I didn't see him a lot after I left the Lab.

I heard that Clinton had a muscle disease when he left work and that was why he left, and I was curious about his muscle disease because of my diagnosis.

I telephoned Clinton and we did some catching up. He sounded glad to hear from me, didn't know I had left work, and he was sick like me. We talked awhile, and I invited him over to visit. Clinton and his wife Reba came over a couple of days after our telephone conversation. Clinton and I visited and talked about old times and old friends. We discussed our muscle diseases, compared symptoms, and vowed to stay in touch to compare notes on our treatments and medicines. After that, we started talking on the telephone about once a week.

Months passed, and I continued to suffer from muscle weakness, dizziness, heart arrhythmias, shortness of breath, and periods of confusion.

I would be driving along, and all of a sudden, I wouldn't know where I was. I had to pull off the road and rest for a while until I got my bearings.

My doctor ordered some breathing tests at South Georgia Medical Center. I arrived at the appointment and they placed me in an enclosed glass cubicle, and told to breathe in and out while the technician measured my activity.

After the test, the technician told me that I had some restrictions somewhere. He asked me some questions about my lifestyle and work history. I answered his questions and he told me that at my age my breathing problems were work related.

It was 1994 and I was 40 years old. I asked him if he was going to put that it was work related in his report. He told me yes. I told him that if he did Oxy probably wouldn't let me go back to work. He told me it was for my own good. As I was driving home with my wife and told her Oxy would blackball me if they got that report.

During the next few months, my health continued to get worse. My feet would swell to the point that I couldn't walk. It was so bad that my wife would have to take me to Gainesville in a wheelchair to receive the injections that would bring the swelling down. I also was having severe headaches, heart arrhythmias, confusion, muscle weakness with pain, and shortness of breath. My liver numbers were also very high.

Clinton Vann was having similar symptoms and not doing well.

It was 1995 and my health was not good, my short-term disability company, Aetna, started sending me notices that they were going to stop my disability payments, and I began suffering with bouts of depression. I decided that I should to see a psychiatrist, so I made an appointment with Dr. Umesh Mhatre in Lake City, Florida.

My appointment with Dr. Mhatre went well. He is a very understanding, compassionate doctor. He talked with me and explained I was suffering from depression and prescribed Prozac and Tranxene.

The meds seem to help some. I started seeing Dr. Mhatre about every three months.

In early spring 1995, we decided to sell our home in Lake Park on the golf course and move down to my father's farm in Jennings. I was afraid if Oxy and Aetna stopped my disability benefits I would lose my home.

We sold our home and purchased a small doublewide mobile home with much lower monthly payments.

My short-term disability ran out, and I had to apply for long-term disability. I also applied for Social Security Disability. My future was looking extremely bleak about that time. Oxy filled my position at work, and I didn't see myself going back to work anytime soon.

That was when I started seriously weighing my options. Clinton Vann and I were doing a lot of research about chemical exposures using the internet. Clinton and I knew about every chemical we had been in contact with over the last 20-25 years.

I called a family friend who was an attorney in Miami, Florida to discuss our findings and seek advice. Henry Ferro was an attorney in Miami, Florida and was a judge there for a while.

I talked to Henry about filing a chemical exposure lawsuit against Oxy. Henry informed me that he would do some research, but thought our only avenue would be through worker's compensation.

A few days passed and Henry recommended a worker's compensation attorney in Ocala, Florida. He discussed the case with her and advised me to make an appointment.

I called Dorothy Clay Sims and we decided to meet at the Waffle House off of interstate 10 in Live Oak, Florida. Dorothy met Clinton and I and discussed our case. She had already prepared the paperwork to file the case, and I was nervous about the whole thing. I really didn't want to sue Oxy, but I didn't know what else to do. I had mixed feelings about suing.

Clinton and I signed the paperwork, and we had a lawyer representing us. This was the beginning of one hell of a fight.

I continued going to my doctors for checkups and meds. I was receiving Dep-Medrol shots regularly but was still having a lot of inflammation and pain in my feet and muscles. Dr. Longley finally prescribed me Methaprednisolone so I could dose myself better during flare-ups.

He also prescribed Hydrocodone for pain as needed. However, Dr. Longley treated me different after I filed the workers compensation case. I don't know why but he stopped sending me progress reports after I filed the case.

Up until then, he sent me progress reports every three months.

He once told me with my wife present, "You will be black balled from industry."

He told me no one would hire me. That pissed me off, and I told him I couldn't work anyway so what did it matter.

I think Oxy had a little chat with Dr. Longley beforehand. He started treat me indifferently because I think he wanted me to find another doctor, but he was the closest to me with his specialty. I think he was afraid of finding himself drawn into the middle of a nasty lawsuit, and maybe, a little afraid of Oxy because they were the big boys in Hamilton County.

Generally, big corporations like Oxy get their executives involved in community affairs as part of they're public relations strategy to make it look like they're part of the family and looking out for the good of the local people. That way, they can get to know and have influence over many people. Therefore, I had my suspicions about the way things were going.

We were in the summer of 1995, and from time to time, I received phone calls from my co-workers checking on me. I received a phone call from Jesse Nash one evening. Jesse was shipping supervisor at Swift Creek Chemical.

We worked together for a short time in 1986. After my transfer to E/P in 1986, Jesse and I were on the same shift. We were also on the emergency response team and fire brigade together.

Jesse and I talked about old times for a while and about my health problems. After a bit, Jesse confessed to me that he was having similar health problems. I shared my doctor's names with Jesse and tried to advise him on how to get a little relief.

I didn't hear from Jesse for several months. That's when his health took a turn for the worse. The word was getting around that Clinton and I had filed a worker's compensation claim against Oxy. Moreover, Jesse was asking a few questions around the company.

About that time, I received a letter in the mail informing me that they denied my workers compensation claim against Oxy. The letter was from Crawford and company, Oxy's workers compensation insurance carrier and service agent. I gave Clinton a telephone call, and he said that they denied his claim.

About this same time, I also received a letter from Social Security that they denied my disability claim. To say the least, things were looking extremely bleak about that time. The only bright spot was that Aetna had approved my long-term disability claim, and at least I would have some income coming in.

I learned later on that Social Security usually denies claims at this level. So, I went ahead and appealed my claim with social security.

I also called Dorothy Sims in Ocala to see where we would go from there. Dorothy wanted to set up a meeting with Clinton and me.

We met with Dorothy and her staff in the fall of 1995. Dorothy explained the process of workers compensation. She said we had a good case but it was also very difficult.

Chapter Eight

Long term chronic chemical exposure is hard to prove. Acute short-term chemical exposure is relatively easy for obvious reasons.

Dorothy gave us a list of things she wanted us to do.

She wanted us to write a brief history of our work careers. She also wanted a list of chemicals and other harmful substances we were exposed to. Then she wanted a list of co-workers or witnesses to these exposures.

Lastly, she wanted us to read a book, "A Civil Action" by Jonathan Harr. I asked why we needed to read this book and she said it would give us an idea of what we were going up against and how difficult it could be.

The book is about chemical exposures making people sick in a town up in Woburn, Massachusetts and the struggle these people had to try and obtain justice. It also gives you explains the struggles of the lawyers fighting a large corporation with unlimited resources. Dorothy said Oxy denied that we were exposed to any harmful substances and were not ill from working there.

When you're ill, it's hard enough just trying to carry on normal life, and large corporations like Oxy know that and know that most people will give up rather than fight.

The meeting with Dorothy left a bad taste in my mouth. She was really compassionate and understanding.

I was starting to become angry. Clinton had given Oxy twenty-seven years, and I gave twenty-one years of loyal service to Oxy. We were both excellent employees with fine records of service. I rose from a sample man in 1972 to an area supervisor managing one third of Swift Creek Chemical in 1993.

The service didn't matter and the fine record didn't matter, we were just nameless, faceless numbers on a multinational corporation's ledger sheet, and no longer seen an asset to some Oxy bean counter. It didn't matter to the corporate bean counters, the executives, and Oxy's shareholders that I had four small children to feed and raise, I was now a liability. If they allowed me to claim workers compensation, it meant that the insurance rates would go up and that meant less profits for the shareholders.

What Oxy didn't know was if a fight is what they wanted, then I intended to give them as good as they gave. Clinton Vann and I knew every little nasty secret they were trying to hide.

When you play with sharks, you have to become one, think like one, and have no compassion or empathy for the adversary. If you smell blood, go in for a kill.

I was born and raised in a small rough lumber house without running water or a bathroom. We hand-pumped the water from the well and carried it into the house. I bathed in a number two washtub with cold water.

Some of my first memories were of working hard on the farm. My dad always told us kids, work hard and you would prosper. I believed in hard work. I was brought-up with a strong work ethic. I worked hard for everything I had, and now I was just a faceless number some corporate bean counter struck a line through – just another expendable employee.

At that point, I knew exactly the type of people I was dealing with and knew there was no reasoning with them – it was kill of be killed.

I honestly and naively thought that the Oxy would take care of Clinton and me.

Clinton was a gentle and kind man. He worked hard at Oxy too and didn't deserve to be treated that way either. We both felt like we were considered just so much trash to toss out on the rubbish heap when they finished using us.

When that revelation hit me, I decided Oxy was going to pay my benefits, or I was going to die trying and do as much damage to them as I could before I died. I knew that I was as tough as they come, and the Oxy boys and their high-powered law firms didn't scare me in the least.

Living back at the farm where I was born and raised seemed to give me even more strength and determination. This was the place I where I started out in life, and just being back there gave me an inner strength and peace of mind.

It was January 1996 when I started writing my brief work history for our attorney. The more I wrote and thought about my career, the more memories started flooding back.

After writing the brief history and naming chemicals I was exposed to, I went to the library and checked out the book, "A Civil Action" by Jonathan

Harr. Dorothy told us we should read the book so we would get an idea of what the future held in store for us.

I read the book from cover to cover and found it very interesting and informative. The plaintiffs in this book were suing W.R Grace and Beatrice Foods, both were large corporations. The book also gave me some ideas on how to help investigate and what to look for to help our case.

Henry Ferro the attorney in Miami that referred us to Dorothy Sims in Ocala called and wanted to file a personal injury lawsuit against Oxy in our behalf. In the case law, he found that we could file a lawsuit against our employer for personal injury if we could prove that we were purposely injured or injured through their actions.

We were sure that our injuries occurred through executive decisions, and we could sue for personal injury.

This opened up a new barrel of worms for Oxy to think about and defend. Henry wanted to test the waters with just one plaintiff at the time, so he filed suit against Oxy just naming Clinton Vann as the plaintiff.

He said that we would soon see how the court responded.

Dorothy called again around March of 1996 and wanted to meet with Clinton and me again to plan a strategy. Clinton and his wife Reba along with me and my wife Gloria headed to Ocala to meet with Dorothy. We both completed our brief work histories and listed chemicals we were exposed to, and we both read the book, "A Civil Action."

I think Dorothy was a little overwhelmed with this case at first, but showed no sign of backing off at that stage. We would come to find that she was a fierce competitor. She told us she was going to assemble a team of legal experts to help with the case. She knew a chemist who was also a lawyer she said would be very helpful.

She wanted Clinton and I to find a doctor or toxicologist to read our histories and do some testing to see if they could find some of those chemical exposures in our bodies, hair, nails, and bones.

She also didn't want to send us to anyone of her choosing for fear it would look like someone she paid to testify in our favor.

We left the meeting feeling like we were starting to get somewhere with our case. Our wives, Gloria and Reba were very supportive. They knew all too well that Clinton and I were suffering with major health problems due to our workplace exposures.

After a meeting, Reba always would say, "We gonna fight'em boys"

Chapter Nine

When we returned home, we started looking for places that did tests for chemical exposures. I found several places, one in South Florida, and the other in Louisiana.

Clinton also found several places, but one seemed to be better than the rest. It was the Environmental Health Center in Dallas Texas. At Dallas, they not only tested for chemical exposures, but they also offered treatments for chemical poisoning.

Clinton and I discussed the different places and decided on the center in Texas.

I called Dorothy, told her what we found, and she thought it was a good choice. Then Clinton and I started planning our trip to Texas. We decided to take the trip in April of 1996.

I called the center and set up appointments, and the center sent us instructions along with an information package.

The information package was very informative and at the time, it impressed me. I felt that maybe we could get some answers there along with a chance to improve our health.

Clinton and I decided to drive rather than fly. Gloria and Reba were going to accompany us on the trip.

We left Florida about April 16, 1996 and headed to Texas. We were driving Clinton's car because it was newer than mine was. We traveled until we were tired, stopped, and rented a motel room for the night.

We arrived in Texas around 18 April and stayed at the Holiday Inn just outside Dallas. We checked in, relaxed a while, and went to bed early because our appointments for testing were early the next morning.

The next morning we headed to the center for our first day of testing. The whole process was to take about a week.

I met with Dr. William Rea the first morning and he outlined what they would be looking for and how. I sent my work history, list of chemicals exposures, and the symptoms to him in advance. I also gave him a list of the diagnosis from each doctor I saw.

The center itself was very clean and professional. There were many patients in the center and some were in very bad health.

I talked to one man from Louisiana who was there with his wife. He told me that there was a spill where they lived, and both his wife and he were suffering adverse health effects due to breathing the fumes. He said that his wife was there for testing and treatment.

I went through a battery of tests for several days. They drew blood, clipped out hair and fingernails. Then they even performed a series of tests for allergies. After all that, I had a second meeting with Dr. Rea about the results.

He said they found n-hexane, benzene, and 11trichloroehane in my blood. My hair analysis showed elevated levels of calcium, zinc, iron, manganese, vanadium, and selenium.

Clinton's results came back a slightly different but very similar.

Dr. Rea also wanted to perform a brain SPECT scan on Clinton and me, so we made the trip across town to the Advanced Metabolic Imaging Center in North Dallas for those tests.

Once there, they directed me to lie down on a table under a machine. Then a technician placed my head in a plastic holder and taped it to the bed so my head wouldn't move. Next, another technician injected me with a radioactive isotope so the brain SPECT machine could see inside my brain.

Clinton went through the same procedure.

We both went back to our motel rooms for a well-needed rest because we were receiving the results of the tests from Dr. Rea the next day. We were finished with our testing and only had to wait on the brain SPECT scan results.

The next morning, we returned to the Environmental Health Center for our final meeting and brain SPECT results.

At that time, SPECT imaging was cutting-edge technology and there were only three like it in the country.

When we met with Dr. Rea, he told me that the brain SPECT results showed a pattern that was consistent with exposures to neurotoxic chemicals. Clinton's results showed the same pattern.

He also stated that that they could slowly remove the toxic chemicals in our bodies through a six-week program.

The program consisted of a strict diet, exercise, sauna treatment, chelation therapy, and other methods depending on the individual case. I told him I would think about it, but it was expensive and I couldn't afford the treatments at that time.

After that, we all loaded up and headed back home to Florida.

I was exhausted, and it had been a long week. We arrived home after about two and half days of traveling. I was sure glad to be back in Florida country and driving down the dirt road that led back home.

I gave Dorothy Sims a phone call when I got back from Texas, and told her the about the testing and brain the SPECT results. Dorothy was very excited and requested a copy right away.

At that time, I thought we had the ammunition to persuade Oxy to pay us our benefits. However, in the meantime, to be on the safe side, I just kept searching for more information on chemical exposure and reading everything I could find on the subject.

The internet offered a wealth of information if you just take time to find and read it.

About that time, I received a phone call from Jesse Nash. He called like clockwork about once a month, just to checkup on my health and well-being.

Jesse, like Clinton and me had a host of health problems himself for quite some time. We talked for a bit, and he said he was at the point where he couldn't do his job anymore.

Jesse said he was going to meet with human resources and discuss taking short-term disability so he could get medical help. I suggested that Jesse give Dorothy Sims a call.

His symptoms were similar to both Clinton's and mine, so told him about our trip to Dallas to the Environmental Health Center and the results. Jesse said that he wanted to talk with Oxy first to see if they would go along with his plans before he talked with an attorney and made an appointment for testing. I wished him good luck with his meeting and health.

It seemed like about everyday, I received at least one phone call from someone asking me questions either who was working at the chemical plant or who worked there in the past.

The word that I was taking legal action was spreading among the workers, and others read about it in the newspaper and were curious.

Dorothy called me one morning, and said she had meetings with several other plaintiffs who worked at the plant. She wanted to know if I knew them. Some of them I knew and some I didn't. She then said that she wanted to have another meeting with Clinton and me along with the new plaintiffs, so we scheduled a meeting.

She spoke to Oxy about our trip to Texas and shared their response with me. Naively, I thought we might have some good news at this time, but that wasn't the case. Oxy didn't budge on their position.

It was a new year, January 1997, and I was hoping that we would settle the case soon. I had been ill and out of work close to four years. I wondered about how much longer it would go on before something happened.

When we finally had the meeting, there were so many people attending, she had to set up a conference room to seat everyone. There were several new lawyers and some new plaintiffs at the meeting.

Billy Baldwin was there. He was someone I knew, but I never worked with him. Billy had leukemia and was in remission after a bone marrow transplant. Several more people were there whom I didn't know but who worked at the plant or used to work there.

Dorothy had a general meeting with the whole group and outlined what the next step would be for the new plaintiffs.

Dorothy instructed the new plaintiffs had to do what Clinton and I did: Write a brief history, list their chemical exposures, etc. She then excused the new plaintiffs and had a private conference with Clinton and me.

Dorothy broke the news to us that Oxy had rejected our workers compensation again, even after we went to Texas and the results were in our favor.

They stated that the claim was too broad, no time frame, no specific chemical, no specific time injured, and on and on. They simply were not going to award us anything at all and that was it, full stop, end of sentence.

Naively, I couldn't believe what I heard. We were going to have to prove this case to win!

Dorothy filed a discovery with Oxy and only received worthless information. I spent hours going through a massive pile of nothing!

I told Clinton we were going to have to dig the dirt up on these bastards ourselves if our case was going to go anywhere because Dorothy simply didn't have the resources to do all the footwork on the case. It was just too broad and complicated.

I knew Oxy's lawyers knew that they could drag this case out for years and exhaust our lawyers' and their resources. They had plenty of money and stables filled with high-powered lawyers on retainer that were going to beat our lawyers into submission if we didn't take the bull by the horns.

I was so damn infuriated that I decided I would start writing letters to OSHA, Florida Department of Environmental Protection, and the EPA under the Freedom of Information Act. I also started calling all three stating what I was looking for and why I was looking for the information. Clinton Vann and I worked together on gathering the data and evidence we needed to push our case ahead.

Chapter Ten

One evening, I received a phone call and it was Jesse Nash. Jesse had a meeting with the human resources people about his health problems.

Jesse told me that they took him in a conference room to discuss the situation and said that before the meeting, they were eating watermelon and never bothered to clean the table.

Somewhat pissed-off, he said, "Those people are a bunch of slobs. There were sticky seeds on the conference table along with drying puddles of watermelon juice – it looked like a bunch of sloppy kids had a watermelon party there."

Jesse told them he needed time off to seek out medical help for health problems. Oxy denied his request and told him he had to come to work or get the ax.

Jesse then flew to Texas to the Environmental Health Center in Dallas Texas for the same tests that I had. He also called Dorothy Sims in Ocala and set up a meeting with her for a worker's compensation case.

I was still seeing my regular doctors about every three months, a rheumatologist, cardiologist, and psychiatrist along with my family doctor regularly to keep an eye on everything happening to me.

At that time, I was taking Vioxx for arthritis, Methlprednisolone for muscle inflammation and pain. I took Metaprolol for heart arrithmias. I also took Hydrocodone for overall pain and Prozac for Transxene for anxiety and depression.

Most of my doctors didn't want to talk much about how I became ill. They just didn't want to be involved with anything other than treating the symptoms and showed no interest in what caused the problems. However, my psychiatrist was the exception.

He had a fine education and was very empathetic. He helped me a lot through the hard times and bouts with depression.

After the way Oxy treated Jesse, he was as angry as we were.

Me, Clinton, and Jesse had at great deal of knowledge about the Oxy operation and inside information from being in management positions for a long time. All three of us started compiling information from OSHA, FDEP, and the EPA.

We were the lead people in the group who knew the most about the whole operation and what to look for to give the lawyers.

Oxy fired Jesse because he brought up chemical exposure at his meeting with them. Jesse also returned from Texas with similar results that Clinton and I received.

Initially, we got together because slowly it dawned on us that we had the same health problems. When I asked about other workers at Occidental, Jesse told me about employees who were sick or dying. It was common to hear about people with brain cancer, lung cancer, stomach cancer, leukemia, bone cancer, and other health problems such as toxic brain syndrome or heart attacks.

Once Jesse wrote, "Joe Crosby, the supervisor who recommended me for a permanent job, died in 1979. He was about forty years old. I heard that his lungs were shot.

"There was another fellow, Buck White. They hired Buck from the same temporary crew as me when I started out at Oxy.

"Ol' Buck developed cancer, and one night, he blew his brains out in a guard shack.

"Now that I look back, I should have figured that something was wrong around there; it seemed like people were sick and dying all the time. I should have known that something wasn't right about that place."

Jesse mainly worked at the sulfuric acid plant and had a few good stories and a good sense of humor about how the told them.

An investigative environmental writer, George Glasser got Jesse to write down a lot of his thoughts because he thought Jesse had a unique way of expressing himself. He loved to use his quotes when he got the chance. George always said that Jesse had a "Wry, sardonic sense of humor."

This is one, I remember well:

"The first safety tip ever given me was in 1979 when a fellow said, 'Don't step in puddles because they might not be water.' After two months

and two pairs of shoes, I determined that he was dead serious. In the sulfuric acid storage area, there was a large brick-lined sump for transferring the acid. Over the years, so much acid was spilled in that area that the ground was totally saturated with sulfuric acid. When the acid percolated down and hit the aquifer or lime rock, a reaction would take place that pushed the earth up. We called it 'heaving.' The heaving was so bad in that area; it pushed huge pumps and the sump right out of the ground. Eventually, we dug out the sump and moved it to another area.

"There was a crack in the ground from heaving. We called it `The Saint Andreas fault.' The crack was about one hundred feet long and a couple of feet wide. One day, the bosses decided to fill the crack with concrete. It looked like a big wedge that kept sinking into the ground as the sulfuric acid dissolved the concrete. After that, they ordered us to dig out the whole area, but we never did reach uncontaminated earth. We just dumped tons of lime in the hole and covered it up.

"At the south loading area, the heaving was the worst I had ever seen. It was so bad that trains got derailed in the yard because the heaving twisted, busted or bent the rails. Overhead, even ten-inch steel beams got bent and twisted from heaving.

" When the ground heaved the wrong way, acid drained away from the sump area, spilled over, ate through the walls and saturated the ground. They called in contractors to clean up. They dug down six feet into the ground but syrupy, black acid was still oozing from the earth.

"The areas were so damned contaminated with sulfuric acid that every time it rained the pH meters in the freshwater ditches went off and triggered red flashing lights. These incidents were happening all over the complex. And all the waters in those ditches eventually flow into the Suwannee River."

While the situation was serious, and as bad as things were for us health-wise, we always managed to find some humor in our sad predicament.

Oxy was the big player in Hamilton County. Essentially, they owned the county and had a lot of power. We always had our suspicions especially when several, possibly incriminating toxicological tests went missing after tissue samples had been sent for testing. Jesse found the whole thing morbidly bemusing and wrote:

"One disabled worker I know had severe testicular problems. One night, he was in so much pain, he went to the emergency room and begged the doctors to remove an inflamed testicle and send it to the laboratory for toxicological testing. The doctors obliged. Later, when he inquired about the toxicology tests, they said his testicle was lost somewhere between the

laboratory and the hospital. A similar mishap befell Karen Hobby after
Bobby died. Tissue test results were "lost" by the hospital.

"Sometimes, I ponder over the fate of that testicle and Bobby's lost
paper work. Perhaps, somewhere in a dumpster or landfill is an enlarged,
inflamed, surgically removed testicle wrapped in Bobby Hobby's toxicology
report. Maybe, it's like the 'sock monster' that resides in every washer-
dryer, our support group has a testicle-and-tissue-snatching gremlin
lurking in the hospital corridors?"

Sometimes, I wondered about Jesse, but as bad as things could
get, he could always picked out the humor in the situation and
made you laugh when you knew you shouldn't.

Clinton, Jesse, and I were the primary force that kept things
together.

Clinton Vann - Jesse Nash - Gary Pittman

Although we were doing most of the legwork on research, the
one thing we knew from our supervisory experience was that it's
important to keep everyone's moral up and keep people updated so
they feel like they're in the loop and part of the team.

We started having support group meetings at my house to talk
about our health problems and our case we had against Oxy. It
started out with me, Clinton and Jesse. We would cook and have a
meal and talk about our research and compare notes. Then we
would send copies of our findings to Dorothy for safekeeping and
review.

Working as a team and having a common goal was good for us because it took our minds off our health problems, and we didn't have the time to wallow in self-pity.

We were a damn good team, even if I say so myself.

Chapter Eleven

When I first started out, I didn't think the situation would start to snowball like it did. At that point, I discovered that a lot more people were ill from the working environment at the Oxy than I could have ever imagined.

Almost everyday, someone told me about co-worker who was ill or of someone who they thought may have been poisoned from working at Oxy.

One day, I heard from a friend about an old friend and co-worker was ill, and in the hospital at Gainesville, Florida. His name was Elmer Mathis.

I knew Elmer and his brother Tommy for years. Both were from my hometown of Jennings, Florida. Elmer worked in the mobile shop at Swift Creek Chemical and had been with Oxy for many years.

I also knew Elmer's wife Bonnie and grew up with her.

Elmer had lung cancer and it was getting worse. I went to see Elmer. I told him about my health problems, and he shared some information with me.

I told Elmer that some of us felt like chemical exposure was to blame for our illness and that I went to Texas to a specialty clinic to be tested. I also shared the results with him.

Elmer just couldn't understand why he had cancer and vowed to fight the disease.

He told me he never smoked, drank, and always tried to live a clean life. I wished Elmer the best of luck and told him to call Dorothy Sims.

He worked in the mobile shop where they repaired heavy equipment. There were diesel fumes, welding fumes, fumes from the chemical plant and a lot of gypsum dust that was radioactive and full of some nasty fluorides.

The gypsum dust was also very high in silica and gave off radon - all of these were bad on the lungs.

Elmer breathed a lot radon gas working in that environment.

When people inhale, radon it decays quickly and gives off tiny radioactive particles. These radioactive particles give off the alpha radiation that damage the cells in the lungs. Long-term exposure to radon can lead to lung cancer.

All the scientists agree that radon causes lung cancer in humans. They say, it's the second leading cause of lung cancer in the United States and kills up to 22000 people every year.

It was the summer of 1997, and there was still no resolution to our case. We gathered volumes of information on violations of occupational health and safety and environmental laws committed by Oxy, especially Clean Air Act violations.

Dorothy told us that Oxy said our chemical list was too broad. She said there should be a chemical common to all these illnesses or the so-called "magic bullet."

Curiously, I thought about that aspect quite a bit, and often asked myself that question over and over again.

What was the common factor – the one chemical that no one in the facilities could escape exposure to and was exposed to daily in large enough quantities to cause illnesses? I answered my own question with "fluorides."

Every plant there emits tremendous amounts of fluoride.

It's part and parcel to the phosphate industry. Phozphate rock is technically called fluorapatite.

Fluorapatite generates silicon tetrafluoride as a pollutant during the reaction with sulfuric acid in the acidulation stage of making phosphoric acid.

Florida phosphate rock contains on average about 3.77% fluoride. The phrase "Fluoride is the primary pollutant of concern" is found throughout EPA phosphate fertilizer production documents.

In fact, one Florida phosphoric acid producer supplied most of the fluorosilicic acid from their pollution scrubbers from its pollution scrubbers to supply most of the Untied States and Canada. The US CDC recommends it as 'drinking water fluoridation agent6 of choice,' mainly because it dirt-cheap, and the companies like the endorsement because selling it helps to recover the cost of running and maintaining the pollution scrubbers.

The EPA liked the idea and in 1983, Deputy Administrator Rebecca Hanmer wrote: *"In regard to the use of fluosilicic [fluorosilicic] acid as a source of fluoride for fluoridation, this agency regards such use as an ideal environmental solution to a long-standing problem. By recovering by-product fluosilicic acid from fertilizer manufacturing, water and air pollution are minimized, and water utilities have a low-cost source of fluoride available to them."*

Fluoride pollution has always been a big problem with the manufacturing of phosphoric acid.

The way to say it scientifically is that the emission of fluorine compounds and dust particles occur during the production of superphosphate. Silicon tetrafluoride (SiF_4) and hydrogen fluoride (HF) are released by the acidulation reaction (addition of sulfuric acid) and they evolve from the reactors, den, granulator, and dryer.

The evolution of fluoride is essentially finished in the dryer. Fluorine compounds are also released from gypsum stacks and evaporation ponds.

Some other Hazardous Air Pollutants (HAPs) identified in the processing of phosphate rock include hexane, methyl alcohol, formaldehyde, methyl ethyl ketone, benzene, toluene, and styrene. They don't do tests for these substances when the environmental protection agencies do emission tests.

Heavy metals such as lead and mercury are also present in the phosphate rock and the phosphate rock is mildly radioactive due to the presence of naturally occurring radionuclides. However, they don't test for these for these emissions either.

The fact is that when you work in the phosphoric acid production, there is no escaping exposure to copious amounts of fluorides. Everyone in and around the complexes breathes it every day - eight to twelve hours a day.

---

* A lot of public health scientists say it reduces tooth decay, and considered by the by the public health community to be one of the "top 10 effective public health measures of the 20th Century." Then they go on to say, "Community water fluoridation provides decay prevention benefits for the entire population regardless of age, socioeconomic status, educational attainment or other social variables."

It's just hard for me to believe that adding toxic, pollution scrubber liquor to the drinking water could be beneficial to the health of living thing.

Most of the sick employees worked in that environment for many years breathing and absorbing these fluorides along with all the other nasty stuff.

When I started focusing on fluorides and hit the jackpot. There was loads of information on the internet about fluoride. There had been many cases of fluoride exposures and lawsuits filed over the years.

When I typed the physical problem and fluorides or sulfides into the search engine, they matched up with everything from memory loss to muscle degeneration. However, we were exposed to many different toxic chemicals, and they all played a role, probably acting synergistically.

According to the monograph for fluorine in CRC Handbook of Chemistry and Physics, all fluoride compounds are toxic to a greater or lesser degree.

I also discovered that use of the word "fluoride" is basically a generic term for fluorine when bound with another element.

When a fluoride compound is inhaled, the fluoride salts react with water (for example, in moist lung tissue), and breaks down into hydrofluoric acid and the other component.

The hydrofluoric acid burns a hole in the lung tissue, leaving the accompanying toxic substance at the damaged site. One toxicologist said it you could liken it to rubbing dirt or injecting a poison into a wound.

One German scientist did research of silicon tetrafluoride, the most common form of fluorides we got a good dose of everyday. He said they were particularly dangerous because they inhibited cholinesterase metabolism. Cholinesterase is an enzyme vital to the functioning of the central nervous system.

Hydrofluoric acid is the most corrosive acid known to science. It causes the most dangerous of all chemical burns because of its high corrosivity and toxicity. A small amount of hydrofluoric acid splashed onto the skin will burn through soft tissues all the way to the bone where the calcium in bone neutralizes it.

According to industrial safety manuals, the treatment of hydrofluoric acid burns is a complex procedure requiring the injection of solutions of calcium chloride into and about the affected areas.

If the burn is on a limb, sometimes to save the person's life the only option is to amputate.

Another researcher into the neurotoxic effects of sodium fluoride said that when toxic fluoride compounds are inhaled, "it's like giving them running shoes. The compounds enter the system and do even more damage than by ingestion alone."

Then there were studies about aluminum fluoride causing presenile dementia and kidney problems.

The information seemed to go on forever.

I was reading many interesting articles and studies when I came across an article in a magazine called "Earth Island Journal" written by a Florida man. The article's title was "Fluoride and the Phosphate Connection.[7]" It was an expose about how America's public drinking water is fluoridated with pollution scrubber liquor from phosphoric acid processing. I was impressed because he really did his homework and knew a lot about the phosphate industry.

He was from St. Petersburg near the Bone Valley phosphate region in Central Florida. There is a lot of phosphate mining and production in that area, and they have major problems with the pollution.

His name was George Glasser, and I decided to give him a call.

It was late 1997 when I first spoke with George. He was an investigative environmental journalist. George and I hit it off from the start as we shared stories about the phosphate industry, and we were a couple of native Florida boys who grew up in living a meager rural life style, which sealed our friendship.

Many of our conversations were about bringing food home to put on the table or just eating beans and rice with a small chunk of bacon chopped into smaller chucks because your mother thought she could fool you into thinking there was a lot of meat in the pot.

Previously, in his younger days, George also worked in factories with dangerous chemicals, and knew what it was like in those environments.

He was very knowledgeable about the history of the phosphate industry, knew the process pretty well, and specialized in writing about the effects of fluoride pollution.

We decided that we could benefit from our shared knowledge.

George also had an interest in the toxic torts aspect and wrote several articles about it in relation to chemical exposures.

---

* See Appendix: *Fluoride and the Phosphate Connection.*

He was extremely interested in the legal action we had filed against Oxy and offered his help in any way he could. Later, he told me – our story was like manna from the gods for an investigative environmental writer, because he was the first person to ever get on the inside and talk to management.

I received a letter in the mail about that time from Dorothy. The court ordered that both parties in the complaint were to enter into mediation and try to come to a settlement. All plaintiffs involved in the complaint were to meet Dorothy and her team at the Holiday Inn in Gainesville, Florida in about two weeks.

Henry Ferro the attorney from Miami already filed the personal injury suit against Oxy with Clinton Vann as plaintiff, and Henry intended to add Jesse Nash and me to the lawsuit later.

I asked Henry why he was waiting, and Henry told me he wanted to see how Oxy was going to react. He said that he intended to add everyone to the personal injury lawsuit that filed workers compensation complaints. However, in the meantime, he wanted Clinton, Jesse, and me to meet with him at the Holiday Inn in Lake City, Florida and attend a press release conference he was holding for the Lake City Reporter about the personal injury lawsuit.

Lebron Miles a reporter news editor wanted to interview us for the story. I rented a conference room and we headed to Lake City for the meeting.

Henry, Clinton, Jesse, and I headed to the conference room and waited for the reporter to arrive.

The meeting and the interview took place in the late afternoon. Lebron knocked on the door and Henry stepped to the door to let him in. I was very nervous and could tell Jesse and Clinton were as nervous or maybe even more nervous than me.

I knew that when this story came out in the newspaper it would rattle the tri-county area of Columbia, Suwannee, and Hamilton.

Occidental was a major employer of these three counties.

Henry started the meeting by explaining the complaints against Oxy to the reporter for the Lake City Reporter Newspaper.

Lebron asked Henry a lot questions and then turned to me and started asking questions. I could tell that Henry had briefed Lebron on the case because he was well prepared with his questions.

Lebron asked me quite a few questions such as where I lived, how long I had worked there, what exposures and many more.

Then he interviewed Clinton and Jesse. He was recording our interviews and so was Henry.

After the meeting, Lebron left and the four of us talked a while.

We all then went home and waited for the shit to hit the fan.

The next morning I got a phone call from a coworker who said that we were on the front page of the Lake City Reporter. I didn't know if that was good or bad, but we had to try and put Oxy in the hot seat, because at that point, Oxy wasn't giving an inch.

The front-page article in the paper read *"3 blame chemical exposure for illnesses, workers' comp claims filed against Occidental, PCS."*

The story went on to tell about us filing the complaints and claiming illness from chemical exposure. The paper quoted me as saying, *"I intend to fight these people down to the wire and I'm not a fighter at heart but now it's a mission."* The article also compared our illnesses to the Gulf War Syndrome affecting some American soldiers who were involved in Operation Desert Storm.

Some believe that soldiers were exposed to chemical nerve agents during the war with Iraq. The article also stated that Venon Lloyd, PCS Phosphates vice president of production could not comment on the claims until he could review the matter.

Lloyd referred the matter to Jim Heppel, the human resource manager at PCS, and he said, *"Based on the facts, it's my understanding that in this case, the workers compensation complaint is still pending, it probably is inappropriate for me to comment on it."*

However, Occidental sold out its phosphate operations to PCS phosphate in 1995. I never worked for PCS and neither did Clinton and Jesse along with some of the other plaintiffs.

The newspaper story made everyone that worked for Oxy, now PCS, aware of what was going on with our claims, and Dorothy received loads of calls after this article was printed.

Central Florida Operations
Processing, Mining, and Gypsum Stacks/Evaporation Ponds

Excerpts from articles

The Peninsula Observer - Jan. 27-Feb. 3, 1969
Air Is Fluoridated

by Ned Groth

> Another major source of fluoride pollution is
> the phosphate industry. Phosphate rock, which is the
> major source of phosphorus, phosphoric acid, and
> phosphate fertilizer, is three to five per cent fluoride. In
> Florida's Polk and Hillsborough Counties, seventeen
> plants are clustered around rich deposits of phosphate
> rock. Fumes from these plants have destroyed 25,000
> acres of citrus trees, and damaged vegetation for fifty
> miles in all directions. Cattle in Polk County have
> suffered from fluorosis and died, and people have been
> afflicted with sore throats, burning eyes, nosebleeds and
> respiratory problems. Millions of dollars in damage suits
> have been filed against phosphate plants.

Tampa Tribune - July 21, 1991

Phosphate waste bypasses federal regulation despite
radioactivity
by Morris Kennedy & Booth Gunter

> TAMPA - Fertilizer companies scour and blast crusty,
> radioactive deposits from filtering equipment, then pile
> the waste on gypsum stacks.

> Contaminated with radium, it is among the most
> concentrated radioactive waste that comes from natural
> materials. Yet the federal government has no rules for its
> disposal.

U.S. News & World Report - June 12, 1995

Sinkholes and Stacks

Neighbors claim Florida's Phosphate Mines are a Hazard

by Michael Satchell

- Eight stories tall, blocking out the sun and swinging a bucket as big as her three-bedroom bungalow, the machine gouged up to 150 tons of earth with each pass.
- Last June, a 15-story-deep sinkhole opened up in an 80 million-ton pile of phosphogypsum waste -- known as a gypsum stack -- at IMC-Agrico's New Wales plant. The hole could be as big as 2 million cubic feet, enough to swallow 400 railroad boxcars... The cave-in dumped 4 million to 6 million cubic feet of toxic and radioactive gypsum and waste water into the Floridan aquifer, which provides 90 percent of the state's drinking water.

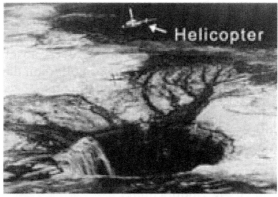

- Since 1990, at least six dams or berms in Florida have failed -- three of them since October 1994. They impound giant clay settlement ponds as well as storage areas for fertilizer-plant waste water that is laced with heavy metals. Billions of gallons of effluent have inundated nearby land, polluting streams and killing fish and other aquatic life. The biggest spill occurred on October 2, when an IMC-Agrico dam burst and released 1.8 billion gallons. On November 19, another of the company's dams failed -- this one only four months old and engineered to higher standards.

- Flat-topped gypsum stacks rise up to 200 feet above the landscape, resembling the mesas of the Southwest. The larger stacks contain up to 80 million tons, about 12 times the mass of the Great Pyramid at Giza.

- While gypsum is relatively harmless (it is often used as a soil conditioner), it is pumped from the fertilizer plants into the stacks in a slurry of waste water that is as acidic as gastric fluid or lemon juice. The effluent contains varying concentrations of 17 heavy metals or other toxic substances, including lead, arsenic, chromium, mercury and cadmium.

- It also contains low levels of radioactivity. Uranium released from the phosphate ore breaks down to produce radium, which contaminates ground water, and radon gas, another carcinogen that is found in high concentrations in the soil of reclaimed mining areas.

- The EPA has declared Florida's 600 million tons of gypsum waste a serious environmental threat, noting in an April draft report: "The ongoing transfer of phosphorus into surface ecosystems constitutes a real and major risk to the long-term health of ecosystems."

Sarasota Herald Tribune - June 14, 1995

Phosphate mining legacy feared
by Waldo Profitt

> "there is a natural and unavoidable connection between phosphate mining and radioactive material. It is because phosphate and uranium were laid down at the same time and in the same place by the same geological processes

millions of years ago. They go together. Mine phosphate, you get uranium."

Tampa Tribune - December 19, 1997

Phosphate industry hits another low

by Frank Sargeant

- Strike the Alafia River off your list of fishing spots. It's gone, dead as a sewer pipe, killed by the carelessness of yet another phosphate company.
- The kill went upriver all the way to the source of the poison, the property of Mulberry Phosphates - a distance of 30 miles. The company allowed some 50 million gallons of phosphoric acid-laced water into the river when a dam on a feeder creek broke.
- The phosphate industry is an important one to thousands of Floridians, and it provides a needed product world wide. But it's time for the legal system to act, if the lawmakers won't, to get the attention of this multibillion-dollar industry and stop, once and for all, the disasters it has inflicted repeatedly on the fish, the wildlife and the residents of the central west coast for so long.

The Ledger - June 21, 2004

Cattle Suffered Due to Fluoride
By Cinnamon Bair

In the 1950s, however, fluoride was nearly disastrous for several agricultural industries in Polk County. Cattle grew gaunt and starved. Leaves on citrus trees turned brown and brittle.

"Between 1953 and 1964 . . . an estimated 150,000 acres of cattle land were abandoned, and 25,000 acres of citrus groves in the county were damaged," Ron Linton wrote about Polk County in "Terracide: America's Destruction of Her Living Environment." "Truck crops were lost, and the commercial gladiolus industry in an adjacent county was blighted."

The problem, scientists determined, was that unhealthy amounts of fluoride were being released into the air by the phosphate industry.

St. Petersburg Times - Apr 12, 1976

Radioactive Fish

South Florida scientists explained that the radioactive sediment of radium and uranuim-bearing calcium fluoride produced by processing phosphate into fertilizer reaches into Hillsborough Bay, an arm of Tampa Bay, from the plant's effluent, and runoff from piles of gypsum, another by-product.

The dearth of marine life near the plant is complete: "no invertebrates, no salt marsh plants, no algae, no fish, no birds feeding there," said Ernest D. Estevez, a doctoral biology student.

NOT ONLY are animals missing, but so is any trace of them, such as shells.

"The high acid content disintegrates them," Estevez explained. "It's possible to find root systems of plants in the mud near the effluent shared off by the acid. It looks like five-o'clock shadow.

"There is no comparable area in Tampa Bay. Even at the height of Red Tide outbreaks, we've always had some living organisms. But not here."

Even farther away from the plant, the study showed, marine life is less plentiful than elsewhere in the bay.

Sam B. Upchruch, a University of South Florida associate professor, said "this is not a crisis, but we need to make some attempt to monitor the radioactivity that may be building up in the bay and in the creatures that live there."

UPCHURCH SAID the radioactive sediment apparently was the first ever detected in the bay, and called for extensive studies to monitor radioactivity throughout Tampa Bay. He said no radioactivity was found in water itself — just on the bottom.

The absence of any marine life in about 100 acres of bay near the ditches that carry the plant's effluent to the bay is largely the work of the heavily acid, heated plant discharges, the scientist found.

Sarasota Herald-Tribune - 9 Feb 1969

CITIES FACING A SHORTAGE OF FLUORIDE ADDITIVE

Special to the New York Times

Published: August 12, 1982

LAKELAND, Fla., Aug. 11— A growing number of cities are facing severe shortages of fluoride additives used in water supplies to prevent tooth decay.

Twelve cities in the West and Middle West, including Seattle, Youngstown, Ohio, and Green Bay, Wis., have been forced to halt their fluoridation programs, according to Arthur Jackson, a public health specialist at the national Centers for Disease Control in Atlanta. In addition, shipments to several other cities, including San Francisco and Washington, have been curtailed by 30 to 50 percent since June...Chemtech is the nation's largest distributor of fluosilicic acid, the compound used by most large water systems for fluoridation.

Sarasota Herald-Tribune - 17 Sep 1966 Sarasota Herald-Tribune - 9 Feb 1969

Phosphate Industry Official Challenges Pollution Article

LAKELAND (AP) — A phosphate industry official Friday said a Life Magazine article citing heavy pollution by the industry in Polk County was "not to be believed."

"Life lives in the past," said Homer Hooks, executive director of the Florida Phosphate Council. "It has relied on old and discredited information."

In a Feb. 7 edition article on pollution, the magazine cites instances of befouled air in New York City, Washington, D.C., East Chicago, Ind., Los Angeles, Missoula, Mont., and Polk County.

The article contends phosphate mines rain heavy amounts of fluoride compounds over Polk and Hillsborough counties and in

the last 20 years have cost citrus growers and cattlemen about $14 million.

"People living there are reluctant to grow vegetables because of this rain of chemicals. Many of them go around all day with sore throats," said the article.

The magazine displayed a photograph of a "fertilizer-producing phosphate plant which lights up the night sky burning off wastes, including fluoride compounds."

"The photo used by Life Magazine is phony," said Hooks, who identified it as a view of the Agrico Chemical Co. plant at Pierce, in lower Polk County.

"Actually the plant shown is a phosphorous operation which does not emit any

fluorides. So the picture is dramatic but false," said Hooks, who speculated that the vaporous cloud over the plant was "steam."

Hooks said the State Board of Health has produced statistics which show that the amount of fluorides emitted by plants in Polk and Hillsborough has decreased from about 18,000 pounds a day in 1961-62 to about 1,500 pounds a day currently. The maximum acceptable rate set by the state agency is 5,537 pounds a day, said Hooks.

The phosphate official said the cattle and citrus industries in Polk County are flourishing, and only one complaint by a ditrusman of damage due to phosphate pollution was received in 1968.

Industry Turns Peace River Into 'Buzzard' Wonderland

PUNTA GORDA '(AP)— Once the sweet smell of cypress sap drifted over the Peace River as it wound through a sleepy Central Florida Wilderness. Hawks wheeled overhead as the flowing waters followed a 75 mile path to the sea, and waterfowl prowled the banks in search of crabs and panfish.

Now, the whirr of buzzards' wings fills the air. The stench from millions of fish rotting in the marshy lowlands that line the nearly lifeless river is gagging.

The Peace River is still, dead, an industrial drainage ditch.

In 10 years it has known no peace.

There have been four major phosphate sludge spills. The last—10 days ago—sent an estimated 2 billion gallons of white slime oozing into the river.

"It's a major ecological disaster," said Norman Young, a biologist with the Florida Game and Fresh Water Fish Commission in Lakeland.

"Twenty-one species of fish are dead, including 11 game species. Wildlife has been displaced — waterfowl and alligators."

Ninety per cent of the panfish, snook, bass, and catfish were wiped out, he estimated.

Restocking will take a minimum of 1,956,000 fish, said

Wayne Stephens, assistant director of the Florida Pollution Control Department.

An earthen dam at Cities Service Phosphate mining pond near Fort Meade ruptured Dec. 3 unleashing a tidal wave of slime. The plant is a division of Cities Service Oil Co.

Cascading phosphate residue flooded Whidden Creek, a nearby swamp, and closed five secondary state roads as it pushed to the river east of U.S. 17.

In spots, it climbed the banks and settled in lowlands, trapping helpless aquatic life.

Fish, tangled in brush as the waters receded, died trying to escape the inevitable, their gills oozing with caustic goo.

Car Pins Tampa Man To Utility Pole

TAMPA, (AP) —Eddie Lowe, 34, was about to enter his auto on the driver's side Saturday morning when he saw another auto approaching at high speed from the rear of his car.

Lowe jumped in front of his own car to avoid being struck by the speeding auto, police said, but was killed when the other car slammed into his and it pinned him against a utility pole.

The river will recover, pollution officials say. It always has. But it will take time.

The offender will pay for damages, too, the state says.

The federal government, state government and some local authorities along the four - county path are preparing to sue.

"But how can you charge for recreational loss; for ecological damage or long term loss in breeding?" asked Stephens.

"It's not possible to assess the diverse loss to the ecological system in the Peace River," a Fish and Game report says.

And what about continuous runoff from heavy rains that will wash more slime back into the stream?

Stephens said cold cash damages would total at least $1 million to restore aquatic life. The City of Arcadia is planning a $500,000 suit for pollution of the Peace River,which it uses as a backup municipal water supply. The National Environmental Protection Agency has asked the Justice Department to take action under an 1898 law that prohibits pollution of navigable waters. And the Florida Department of Natural Resources is studying effects on saltwater fish and marine life in Charlotte Harbor at the river's mouth on the Gulf of Mexico.

St. Petersburg Times - 7 Jun 1979

The strip miners are dying

In the clay beds beneath Central Florida, uranium ore is buried with the gray phosphate pebbles that are strip-mined to make agricultural fertilizers.

Now, the first phosphate miners in Polk and Hillsborough counties have begun dying of cancer. In the past five years at Brewster Phosphates Co., 16 of 214 employees who worked in the mine for 15 years or longer have developed cancers. Eight of them died.

ALTHOUGH that alarming situation might have been hidden indefinitely, the Brewster Co., jointly owned by American Cyanamid and Kerr-McGee Corp., voluntarily disclosed Tuesday that its employee cancer rate is more than four times the national average. A medical research team from the Johns Hopkins School of Public Health in Baltimore has been employed to determine whether radiation is the cause.

Brewster's conduct in this case and its announced intent to keep the investigation open to public view is a commendable exception to the record of the phosphate industry.

During 50 years of intensive strip mining in Polk and Hillsborough, the industry has rarely displayed high standards of corporate responsibility.

ABOUT 20 multinational corporations have despoiled the land and polluted the air and water on a massive scale. Any cleanup measures in the industry's dirty operation usually have been forced by governmental regulation.

With the growing knowledge of radiation hazards, it is difficult to understand why only four of the 18 companies in the Florida Phosphate Council, a trade association for the industry, have offered regular physical examinations to their employees. The lack of medical records will make it more difficult for scientists to document the health risk.

But the mysterious long-term effects of excessive radiation are a national concern. We trust that the Florida Phosphate Council and all the mining companies will make a concerted effort to determine — and correct — the health hazard for the industry's 12,000 employees.

Chapter Twelve

Shortly after the meeting and press release with Henry and the Lake City Reporter, we traveled down to Gainesville to our mediation with Oxy.

Earlier, the judge ordered that the parties in the lawsuit attempt to come to a settlement through mediation. Dorothy Sims our workers comp attorney was there with her staff and Oxy's attorneys were present.

The mediation procedure addressed each case individually.

Dorothy and a client would go into a room where Oxy's attorneys attempted negotiate a settlement.

Clinton went in ahead of me, and I waited for him to emerge.

After about thirty minutes, Clinton came out and gave me a frustrated look, and I asked how it went. Clinton threw his hands up, shook his head, and said it was a joke. He said that they didn't want to settle, it was all just show to satisfy the judge's order to mediate.

I asked him what they offered. Clinton told me, five thousand dollars. I was next and knew that it wasn't going to be pretty because I wasn't going to settle for five grand when I already invested a lot more than that in pushing the case forward.

Dorothy and I went in to see if we could negotiate a settlement. Dorothy and Oxy's attorneys talked about the claim and our figures on how much the settlement should be.

The attorneys for Oxy offered me five thousand dollars. I looked at Dorothy and she knew what to reply, she said "no way."

I couldn't take five thousand dollars. I had over ten thousand dollars of my own money in this case already counting the trip to

Texas for testing. The brain SPECT alone cost five thousand dollars. So, we packed up and went home.

I knew we were going to have to hit these people hard to make them want to settle. I started thinking of a new strategy.

I went home and thought about the case a lot. I had several ideas that might help. However, Oxy had several huge law firms on their payroll, and we were going to have to fight fire with fire.

I called George Glasser to tell him about our experiences with the mediation. We communicated with each other about once a week and emailed each other information pertaining to the case.

I sent Dorothy so much research already that she had asked me to slow it down a little.

I talked to George, and he wanted to write an article. He had several influential environmental publications that he wrote articles for on a regular basis and said the editors would jump on the story because of the legal and human angle. He said there would be no problem getting it published, and the magazines had large international readerships.

I thought it was a great idea.

He asked me to write a short account on this whole ordeal from the start to where we were at with the case. He also asked me to ask Clinton and Jesse to do the same. I also asked Billy Baldwin to write a story too.

Our wives Gloria, Reba, Joanne, and Charlotte were going to write an account from their point of view. All of our wives supported us whole-heartedly.[8]

The whole bunch of us went to work writing our stories.

We gained a lot of local support from the tri-county area from the newspaper article but we needed broader exposure to put pressure on Oxy, and that's what George could do for us. He could take to a much broader audience and the publications influential people read.

While we were all beavering away writing for accounts for George, Dorothy called me one morning and wanted me to come down and sort through some more boxes of discovery evidence. I had already gone through boxes and boxes a few months before.

Turns out that she wanted me go through the boxes and mark and tag anything that we could use as evidence in the case, which

* See Appendix: Wives' Accounts – Excerpts from *Death in the Air.*

was very time consuming. She also wanted me to go to Elmer Mathis' deposition with her.

Elmer was in North Florida Regional Hospital in Gainesville and was not doing well at all. Elmer's lung cancer and was getting worse and they didn't expect him to be around much longer.

Gloria and I met Dorothy at the hospital in Gainesville for Elmer's deposition. Oxy's attorneys were there along with the stenographer. Dorothy asked Gloria to video Elmer's deposition.

The deposition began and Dorothy started asking Elmer questions about his job at the plant.

Elmer answered her questions prompt and honestly. He talked about the fumes, dust and diesel exhaust. He was very weak and pale lying in his hospital bed.

Gloria became ill during the deposition and couldn't continue videotaping after about twenty minutes, so one of Dorothy's assistants had to take over video duties.

Gloria wasn't feeling well that morning anyway. Gloria told me she was going to wait in the car.

Elmer's deposition continued, and sometimes he would hesitate before he answered a question. The Oxy lawyers took advantage of his weakened state with aggressive questioning, and it seemed to be intimidating to Elmer. He was also on some heavy-duty medications for pain, but he did the best he could under the circumstances.

The Oxy lawyers were a couple of smug, smart asses. They knew if they rattled Elmer, he would probably blow the deposition. They also knew that he wouldn't live long enough to appear in court, so they took full advantage of the situation.

A couple of times, I was tempted to give them a good whack.

However, Elmer did his best under the circumstances and knew that some of his testimony confirmed some of the health hazards at the plant we alleged in the complaint.

When the deposition finally ended, I visited with Elmer and Bonnie a while. I later wished Elmer well and headed to the car.

It was a long walk back to the car from Elmer's room, I knew Elmer was dying and that was the last time I would see him.

I was very weak myself due to the muscle disease and had to take several rest breaks on my way back to the car. When I finally arrived at my car, Gloria was waiting and still not feeling well.

When I got to the car, I asked Gloria if she was feeling any better. She told me that she just couldn't look into Elmer's face anymore. She told me that she kept thinking that it could be me lying in that bed and she started crying.

I told her that I would be ok and maybe Elmer would pull through trying to make her feel a little better.

After Gloria gained her composure, she said, "You wouldn't believe what I just saw?" She said the two company lawyers had parked in front of us about two rows down. Then Gloria said that they were laughing and doing high fives on the way to their cars after the deposition.

I couldn't believe what she told me. I was near tears leaving Elmer's room and watching him testify on what was to be his deathbed. At that point, I knew exactly what kind of people we were dealing with.

Gloria and I returned home talking about the events of the day and the case.

A few days passed and I received a call from George Glasser. He had finished the article and wanted me to read it.

He emailed the article over and I started reading it. The name of the article was "Death in the Air."

I really got excited reading what George wrote. He had captured the lawsuit and made it come alive on paper.

He included stories from a lot of the plaintiffs in the lawsuit and it gave different perspectives from different view. It was filled with facts about fluoride and the damage the phosphate industry has inflicted on the environment. It was simply a good piece of work.

He asked me if I thought it would be ok with everyone if he went ahead and got the ball rolling with publishing it.

After what I saw at Elmer's deposition, I told George to go for it. I told him we were going to have to give it everything we could muster to get any justice.

George already had several respected environmental magazines he shopped the story around to that wanted to publish it. However, lawyers for one publication foresaw a problem. According to them, it was incendiary story, and although George had all his ducks in a row as far as sources and credible citations for the article went, the magazine could still find itself facing a lawsuit or injunction.

They put their heads together realizing that there was a two-month lead-time on publication, and decided the best approach was to publish it on the Internet because then it would be in the public domain.

The strategy behind the plan was that once on the Internet, there wasn't much the defendants could do legally to get it off. And if by some chance, Oxy's lawyers got wind of it before publishing and tried to file an injunction to stop publication, they couldn't get it in a Florida court that was friendly to phosphate industry. It meant that they would have to go to a Federal Court, which could take years before the case they heard the case.

At the time, I didn't realize how well connected George was; he consulted with a lot of top toxicologists, researchers, and a few good environmental lawyers about his articles before publishing them.

George also had a large international following that read his articles. A lot of his work is still up on the Internet all over the place, and people still quote from the articles.

Shortly, after he posted the article on the Internet, people were contacting me from all over the place, and before the Earth Island Journal and SunCoast Eco Report published a shortened article, it was republished on a lot of websites and other magazines around the world.

After he published the article, George started getting nasty phone calls in the middle of the night. He told me he was used to it and that sort of attempted intimidation came with the territory. He said, "Anyway, there ain't much they can do after the cat is out of the bag except try to scare me away from doing a follow-up on the story."

Chapter Thirteen

All of the plaintiffs involved in the lawsuit tried to get together at least once a month to talk about our health problems and share ideas about the lawsuit.

I don't know if the others were aware, but I knew all too well that we were going up against a mammoth organization with lot to lose.

Occidental Chemical was the parent corporation of Hooker Chemical Corporation. Hooker was in the most part responsible for Love Canal catastrophe having disposed of 199,900 tons to chemical waste at the site, and they were no strangers to litigation.

The Love Canal story, to put it simply was one of the most appalling environmental tragedies in American history. It was a small area used for a hazardous waste disposal site by Hooker Chemical Corporation and some other companies since the 1920s. In the early 1950s, Hooker sold the site to the city with a disclaimer for $1.00.

In the late 1950s, developers built about 100 homes and a school on and around the site.

In 1958, there was a record rainfall. Corroding waste-disposal drums broke up through the ground, and the trees and gardens started turning black and dying. A swimming pool popped up from its foundation and was afloat on a small sea of toxic chemicals.

All around the development there were puddles of toxic, corrosive, and noxious substances – some were even on the school grounds.

The air was permeated with the smell of chemicals.

The Children returned from playing with chemical burns on their hands and faces.

The New York State Health Department found alarmingly high rates of miscarriages and birth defects.

In 1979, the Love Canal case was the largest environmental complaints ever lodged by the Federal government against a major corporation. The Department of Justice acting on behalf of the Environmental Protection Agency filed four suits against Hooker Chemical and Occidental Petroleum for $117.5 million in clean up costs alone.

In the end, Oxy paid the USEPA $129 million and was out of pocket a total of $200 million for damages and settlements, not including court cost and the millions they spent defending themselves.

St. Petersburg Times - 21 Dec 1979

Firm sued for $124-million for toxic pollution in Love Canal

United Press International

WASHINGTON — The government Thursday sued the Hooker Chemical Co. to force it to spend $124-million cleaning up New York's Love Canal and three other chemical dump sites in the most expensive punishment yet sought in such a case.

The Environmental Protection Agency (EPA) said the suits represent a landmark attempt to prove that a company that did something years ago — 30 or more years back in Hooker's case — is still responsible for the lingering effects.

It also marks the first time the EPA has sought to make a company pay for medical studies of persons exposed to chemical dumps. The suit seeks $2-million a year for research on Love Canal residents.

The four civil suits were filed Thursday by the Justice Department against Hooker and its parent firm, Occidental Petroleum Corp., in federal court in Buffalo, N.Y.

HOOKER PRESIDENT Donald Baeder said the suit is "unwar-

in congress

ranted and will be vigorously resisted."

Barbara Blum, deputy EPA administrator, told a news conference the suits constitute the costliest relief ever sought by the agency in a chemical dumping case. She declined to say whether the government was considering the possibility of criminal prosecution in addition to the civil suits.

Hooker has already been hit by and former Love Canal residents.

Ms. Blum said the suits "should serve notice to those who generate or handle hazardous wastes that these kinds of dangers no longer will be tolerated by the American public. The day of discarding hazardous materials indiscriminately and haphazardly is over."

IN THE LOVE Canal area, 82 toxic chemicals, including 12 that cause cancer, were identified in sur-

face soils, home air and basement sumps, the suit said.

The other sites the suits seek Hooker to restore include: the "S" area landfill, where chemicals threaten the city's drinking water supply; the "Hyde Park" site where the deadly chemical dioxin has been found in a creek; and the 102nd Street area where "children playing on the land-fill have been burned by exploding fire rocks," the suit said.

The suits filed Thursday seek $117.7-million in cleanup costs and an additional reimbursement to the federal government of $7-million it spent on emergency measures at Love Canal.

Hooker Chemical is also in litigation in Florida courts involving charges the firm knew and approved of pollution violations at the company's plant in White Springs.

The state is now suing Hooker for $8-million, alleging that the plant knowingly released phosphate and flouride into the relatively unspoiled Suwanee River.

Knowing the size and power of the machine we were up against and the odds against us winning the case; it was hard for us to trust anyone, and at times not even our lawyers.

I knew Occidental had the power to buy and intimidate people and pay off a jury if they wanted to. They could even cause my lawyers problems. They gave money to political candidates, and I was sure that they even had influence over the judges hearing our case.

All of us knew that we were alone in the fight and couldn't really depend on anyone, except one another.

We went up against a mammoth corporation with the resources to hire the best attorneys in the world, hire the best public relations agencies, buy off politicians and judges, and that realization gives a person a real sense of smallness.

However, I was determined to get some sort of satisfaction and obsessed with the lawsuit; it was all I could think about night and day.

Jesse and Joanne Nash were going to host our next meeting. We all traveled down to Lake City to Jesse's place for our meeting.

The group had been to the mediation in Gainesville, Florida together and all of us came away knowing that they were offering up peanuts for a settlement. One person brought up an interesting question. He asked, "What if Oxy offers me something I can accept?"

I walked to the front and said, "We are all fighting this battle together trying to support each other as much as we can, but if you get a settlement that satisfies you then by all means take it.

"We're all individual cases in this work comp suit even though we help each other as a group."

We all agreed that people had to make his or her own decision that would fit their individual circumstances.

We all had a wonderful meal and a good meeting.

Shortly after Elmer's deposition, he passed away. Elmer's passing made us all think of how short this life really is.

I attended Elmer's funeral and witnessed his burial. I will always remember and visualize him giving his deposition at the hospital.

The Lake City Reporter put Elmer's death on the front page. The story read *"Chemical Exposure Claimant Dies At 52."*

The story told about Elmer's chemical exposure claim. Oxy had no comment nor did they offer any condolences.

Several days passed, and I received a phone call from Dorothy Sims.

Dorothy was still working hard on the case, and she felt we were making progress, but it was slow go. She also said that she was going to take Bobby Hobby's deposition and wanted me to attend to help her with the list of questions.

Bobby was a mechanic in several plants that I supervised. Bobby was a good boy and a hard worker.

Gloria and I loaded up and went to Ocala for the deposition.

Dorothy also asked Jesse and Clinton to attend. We arrived in Ocala and went straight to Dorothy's office where the deposition was to take place. The Oxy lawyers at Bobby's deposition were the same ones that were at Elmer's deposition.

Bobby had multiple myeloma, a bone cancer, and undergoing chemotherapy at the time.

I arrived early and had a few questions written down on a sheet of paper for Bobby to answer.

One question was about if he knew anything about some sick cows and the other was about the old super acid plant scrubber.

Dorothy asked Bobby a lot of questions about his job, his length of service, exposures and more.

When we were nearing the end of the deposition, Dorothy asked Bobby about the sick cows.

I think Dorothy was a little reluctant at first to ask Bobby my questions, but she also knew I had something in mind that could be important to the case.

After a little hesitation, Dorothy asked, "Bobby do you know anything about rounding up some sick cows?"

Bobby said, "Yes mam, I sure do."

The Oxy lawyers were frantically wriggling in their seats.

One lawyer objected, and Dorothy said, "Continue Bobby."

Bobby stated that he and several more mechanics went out in the middle of the night and rounded up cows with a company truck. Then he said that the cattle were suffering, severely burned and were about dead because there had been a sulfur dioxide stacking release incident that destroyed crops and burned the cows for miles around the plant – and even dissolved asphalt shingles on people's houses.

Also in Bobby's deposition, he said that workers on his shift were unequivocally told to keep their activities on that night secret.

Bobby and the crew were cleaning up the results of the 1986 horrific sulfur dioxide release incident that caused damage for miles around the plant, but Oxy never notified the FDEP or EPA and the incident went unreported.

When sulfur dioxide comes in contact with ambient moisture in the air, it forms sulfuric acid which is some pretty nasty stuff. The cattle's hides and lungs received acid burns from coming into contact with and inhaling the airborne sulfuric acid.

Most of the farms in the area were small, and many of the people had relatives who worked for Oxy, so they simply paid them off with a little bit more money than their losses. Consequently, they kept their mouths shut and Oxy got away without any bad publicity or fines

When Bobby and some co-workers were helping clean up the mess in the middle of the night, I think they probably shot the cattle and either buried them or dumped them in an acidic evaporation pond so the evidence would simply disappear after a few weeks.

He didn't say much about that, but he said enough to send Oxy's lawyers into an apoplectic fit.

After Dorothy had a little yelling session with the Oxy lawyers the deposition continued.

The next question was, "Did you ever help prepare the super acid scrubber for testing at Suwannee River Chemical?"

Bobby answered, "Yes mam."

Dorothy asked, "How?"

Bobby answered, "We would disconnect the pond water lines to the scrubber and connect fresh water lines and then fill the scrubber with women's sanitary napkins."

Dorothy asked Bobby to explain and Bobby said they couldn't pass a stack test without those modifications. He said that after the stack test, they would remove the fresh water lines and take the sanitary napkins out.

All Oxy lawyers could say was "Object! Object! Object!"

It was hilarious watching those lawyers go at it, and the Oxy lawyers were frustrated to the point of having a cerebral hemorrhage.

After the deposition was over, I watched the Oxy lawyers go to their cars. I can tell you one thing for sure; they weren't laughing and weren't giving each other high fives like they did when they were badgering poor old Elmer on his deathbed dying of lung cancer. They looked like they were getting ready to attend their own funeral services.

That was a real satisfying experience watching those two get taken down to size. I took great personal satisfaction in knowing that when it got back to the executive boys at Oxy, they'd be sending their secretaries out to get antacid for their bleeding ulcers in hopes that lawyers' secretaries hadn't got there first and bought out the stock.

I returned home and rested for a day or two just thinking and patting myself on the back for extracting a little posthumous revenge for Elmer.

The courts moved Clinton's personal injury case to Federal Court, and I knew I didn't want to be going there because large corporations can milk a law firm dry in Federal Court.

Henry Ferro was an old family friend, but he just moved to Ocala was a one-man law firm.

He was handling our cases at the time, and Ferro was using Clinton's case to test the waters.

I called Henry and told him I was going to search for a new lawyer to represent me on the personal injury case. Henry told me to go ahead, he understood.

I had to find a good strong law firm to represent me. I started researching case law and looking for a case similar to mine. I must have looked through five hundred cases, and I was learning a lot about toxic tort law - the hard way.

> *A commission of intentional tort is conduct necessary to remove employer's workers compensation immunity. To fall within intentional tort exception to exclusive remedy provision of worker's compensation act, employer's behavior must have been so egregious as to exhibit deliberate intent to injure or engage in conduct which is substantially certain to result in injury or death.*

After several days of exhausting research, I finally found a case that was almost identical to mine, and the attorneys for the plaintiff were in Jacksonville, Florida only 90 miles from my home.

The law firm was Boyer, Tanzler, and Boyer. I did some research on the firm, and they had a triple A rating.

Tyree A. Boyer was an elderly lawyer that had once been a judge on the fifth district court of appeals. Hans Tanzler was a reputable lawyer and ran for governor of Florida in 1975.

Tyree W. Boyer was the driving force representing the case I found in case law similar to mine on chemical exposure.

It was 1998, and I finally found the law firm I thought could win my case. I just had to sell them on it.

Early one morning, I called the law firm of Boyer, Tanzler and Boyer and told the lady on the phone that I needed them to represent me in a personal injury lawsuit. She told me that she would connect with another person.

Another woman came on the line and told me that she screened the calls to evaluate the potential plaintiffs. I found out later she was a lawyer too.

She asked me a lot of general questions and then many more about my complaint.

I told her that I needed their firm to represent me in a personal injury lawsuit.

She told me it sounded like workers compensation to her. I told her that I had researched the case law on my case, and it was almost identical to Cunningham v. Anchor Hocking Corp., and said that I would like to set up an appointment to talk with Tyree W. Boyer.

At that time, Boyer, Tanzler, and Boyer was the only law firm in Florida to win a chemical exposure case of this type.

She told me to hold, and before long, she came back and made an appointment for me to talk with Tyree Boyer, but it would be in about ten days.

After the initial meeting, I returned home and learned that Bobby Hobby passed away. It didn't take long for the cancer to finish Bobby.

I was an honorary pallbearer at Bobby's funeral along with Clinton Vann.

The funeral was very sad. Bobby left behind a wife and several small children. I was starting to think we were all going to die before we saw any justice.

I knew that somehow I had to continue on pursuing the case. I was very tired and weary, but something kept giving me the strength to keep going. There were too many people counting on me. I prayed about the case often, and that God's will would be done.

Chapter Fourteen

It was time to travel to Jacksonville, Florida for my meeting with Tyree Boyer. I had everything packed in my briefcase for the presentation.

I knew that I had to do a good job selling this case because time was running out for us. We left early in order to find our location. The law offices were in downtown Jacksonville across from the federal courthouse.

We arrived and found a parking place about a block from Tyree's office. I was very nervous and knew we needed this firm to represent us.

Boyer, Tanzler, and Boyer was the law firm that successfully litigated the case that I found, Cunningham v. Anchor Hocking Corporation.

In that case, the plaintiff alleged an intentional tort based on the following facts. The employer had deliberately diverted a smoke stack so that dangerous fumes would flow into rather than outside of the building.

1. *The employer would periodically turn off the ventilation system.*
2. *The employer had removed the manufacturers warning labels on toxic substances.*
3. *The employer misrepresented the toxic nature of the substances involved.*
4. *The employer misrepresented the effectiveness of safety equipment and the danger involved.*

My case was similar to this case, and I had to make Tyree see this.

As we approached the office and there was a lot of activity.

The front of the old building was old but elegant. We went inside and there was old antique furniture all around. An oldish gentleman greeted us and told Gloria and I to come into his office. He said, "How can we help you today."

He was very friendly and down to earth and made me feel welcome. I thought he was some kind of greeter until he introduced himself as Tyree A. Boyer.

He was head of the law firm and treated us like old friends. I liked this firm from the start. I told him I had an appointment with Tyree W. Boyer at 0930 hours. He told me to have a seat and he would let his son know I was there.

Plaintiffs and lawyers were coming and going; it was a bustling law firm. That was a good sign to me. A woman came and showed Gloria and I into Tyree's office.

Tyree was a man that looked about fifty-five years of age. He was a large sturdy looking fellow and well dressed. His office was well organized. He offered Gloria and I a cup of coffee. I declined the coffee and was anxious to get started.

Tyree had a folder in front of him and had reviewed the information I gave the screening woman on the phone. He reared back in his chair and said you know it is extremely difficult to prove a chemical exposure case.

He was talking very loud and seemed aggravated. I thought for a split-second that he was going to send me packing. I told him that I knew it was difficult to prove, and I had been working and fighting this case for over three years. I also told him that with a good group of lawyers we could win.

Then I asked him to take a quick look at the brief history on my work career and exposures. He accepted my offer and started reading. When he finished reading it and told me, it looked like a work comp case to him, but complimented me on my brief history.

I then told him I had researched case law and found Cunningham v. Anchor Hocking Corp and my case was similar and thought it had merit. Tyree smiled and said, "You found that case?"

I answered, "Yes and it's similar to mine."

He smile faded and told me, "That case was a nightmare and we spent countless hours on that case."

I could tell he was thinking about taking on my case. He asked me if I was alone in the case and I told him no.

I said there are many others that will join in with us to try and get justice. Tyree said, "We might can do a class action on this case."

I quickly told him no that I didn't want to do a class action. He asked me why, and I told him the lawyers get all the money and the plaintiffs get chicken feed.

That pissed Tyree off and we argued a little while. After all was said and done, I could tell he respected me and might have even liked me a little bit.

He ended the meeting by telling me he wanted to think about it a few days and discuss it with another lawyer that might partner with him if he decided to take the case. I pushed him for a date to notify me. He told me, "I need a week to think about it."

We shook hands, and I felt like he was going to take the case, but I still wasn't sure.

I returned home hoping Tyree and his firm would take my case. They had the expertise and notoriety to take give Oxy a run for their money.

I received a call from Dorothy shortly after I returned home. She had made an appointment for Clinton and me to see a doctor in Tampa Florida. He was at the University of South Florida and Dorothy made an appointment for us for an electromyogram[9] and evaluation.

Clinton and I decided to go together with our wives. We headed to Tampa and was used to this by now, we traveled together to Texas in 1996 for testing.

We arrived and they performed an electromyogram on Clinton and me along with several other muscle tests. I don't think much became of it, and I never heard the results.

After returning home, I traveled to Jasper in my home county to search records of complaints against the Oxy in the courthouse. I figured there had to be some records because the Oxy was located there. I found several lawsuits that were against the Oxy, but most were sealed so I couldn't see the details of the suits. One was the Morgan case where crops and cows were damaged and some relief was provided, but the amount was private.

I reported all of these to Dorothy and continued doing research. I had also received documents from OSHA and the Florida Department of Environmental Protection (FDEP) through the freedom of information act. There were only twenty inspections at the plants between 1973 through 1996. However, there were numerous citations of different types.[10]

There were several reports of hospitalized injuries as well as burns and fatalities in the OSHA report. There were many violations in the FDEP reports also.

There were failed smokestack tests of the SPA evaporators and C phosphoric acid plant. A stacking start up of sulfuric acid plants led to fines

* An electromyogram (EMG) measures the electrical impulses of muscles at rest and during contraction.

* See Appendix.

for damaging plants with more agricultural damage. There were also fines levied at $575,000 dollars for misrepresenting environmental data.

Gainesville Sun - 8 Jan 1987

Occidental sued by state officials for April leak

The Associated Press

JASPER — Occidental Chemical Co. has been sued by state air-pollution officials for $131,000 in fines and an unspecified amount in damages over an April accident that resulted in chemical burns to crops and trees in Hamilton County.

The lawsuit filed by the state Department of Environmental Regulation caught Occidental officials by suprise on Tuesday.

"It comes while we are in the process of productive negotiations with the state and are close to a settlement," said Artie Lynnworth, an Occidental spokesman.

The suit, filed Monday in Circuit Court in Hamilton County, contends a cloud of sulfur dioxide was released as a result of a poor start-up operation at the sulfur plants at a phosphate mine near White Springs in north-central Florida.

Three sulfuric acid plants were put back in operation at the same time, the lawsuit said, which created an un-

usually high level of emissions.

A temperature inversion kept the emissions close to the ground and an acid cloud, a mile wide and five miles long, destroyed wheat and tobacco crops west of the mine. It caused the leaves of trees to turn brown and burned the eyes of residents in about 20 households.

The lawsuit seeks the the number of claims made by residents and a record of damages paid by the company.

Last month, Occidental rejected a settlement proposed by state negotiators in a proposed consent order, but said the door was still open for more talks.

Occidental attorney Lawrence W. Curtin of Tallahassee said he was under the impression that an out-of-court settlement was near.

"I have not seen the suit. Obviously, we now are going to have to sit down and see what we can do next," he said.

I forwarded all this information to Dorothy for evidence of exposure for our cases.

About that time, Jesse, Billy Baldwin, and I reported the Clean Air Act violations to USEPA Criminal Investigations Division.

The leading EPA investigator told us that an investigation was underway and that they would interview us. Four months later, when I gave him a call, the investigator claimed that he didn't remember my name or anything about an investigation.

I got very angry and pressed him about the case, he finally admitted that the case had been assigned to the EPA office in Jacksonville, Florida.

Even FDEP investigators told me that an investigation was imminent. However, when Jesse telephoned the FDEP and they too claimed that they had no recollection of talking to me.

They advised Jesse to file a complaint with the EPA. When Jesse told me that there was no record of our case, all I could say was, "Looks like they want to bury the case along with us."

By then we should have known what the game was all about by then. It seemed like no one wanted our case to see the light of day.

It was as if almost everyone we contacted had something to hide or I thought that the Oxy people were either buying them off or something. When someone at the EPA says that they don't remember a case, then backtracks. Well, at that point, I definitely smelled the distinct aroma of dead rats rotting in the woodwork.

Chapter Fifteen

By that time, our lawsuit received media attention in newspapers and on the Internet with George Glasser's article *"Death in the Air" "Occidental Exposures - Gary's Story."*

In 1998, I received a phone call from Channel 20 news in Gainesville, Florida. The television station wanted to interview me about the lawsuit. We set up a time and date for the interview. They were going to hold the interview at my home outside Jennings.

In the meantime, I called Jesse and Clinton so they could attend if they wanted. I also called Billy Baldwin and Bobby Hobby's widow Karen Hobby.

On the day of the interview, we all gathered at my home. The television station Channel 20 team from Gainesville, Florida came and did a good interview with us all included.

It was a good piece, they had aerial shots of the chemical plants, and the interviews sounded good.

I thought the interview could only help us get the word out and continue to put pressure on Oxy with negative exposure.

I was learning fast that if you're involved in a big lawsuit, you have to get into the public relations game and learn how to use the media. Big corporations don't like getting bad publicity, and companies like Oxy don't want stories to get out about their poisoning everybody with pollution because it just brings on more toxic tort lawsuits.

Later on that same week, I received a phone call from Jacksonville, Florida. Boyer Tanzler and Boyer wanted to meet with me and wanted me to bring other interested plaintiffs that suffered from chemical exposure.

I informed the group of the news and anyone interested to meet with me at the law firm on the date specified. I felt they were going to take the case and was ready to get started. I also asked Clinton Vann to come along although I knew Henry Ferro was still representing him. I felt that Clinton could sign on with Tyree and our group if he chose to.

All the interested people traveled to Jacksonville for the meeting with the firm.

We arrived and sat around a long conference table. Tyree and several more men entered and Tyree spoke to the group. He told everyone that our case was a very difficult and expensive case to litigate. He also stated that a main reason you bring a complaint against a defendant to try to reach an adequate settlement for the plaintiffs. "The last thing you want to do is go to trial because the outcome is a toss of the coin."

He then told us that the firm had decided to take our case on a contingency basis and explained that it could be years before we might reach a settlement.

Next, Tyree introduced us to the head of another law firm in Jacksonville. His name was Howard Coker and his firm was going to partner with Tyree on this case.

Howard Coker was the sitting president of the Florida Bar at the time. His firm just litigated a chemical exposure case and was successful.

We discussed the case some and Tyree asked Howard what he thought, and Howard placed his finger beside his nose, sniffing, and said, "I smell money."

The firm had the complaint they were going to file in the State Court in Duval County, Florida already prepared; it read Gary Owen Pittman et al plaintiffs vs. Occidental Chemical Corporation et al.

The complaint was for intentionally caused personal injuries. There was a partial list of the known chemicals in the complaint. The complaint also read:

1. *Count 1 Battery,*
2. *Count 11 Fraud and Deceit,*
3. *Count 111 Strict Liability Anti-Pollution Statutes,*
4. *Count IV Intentional Infliction of Emotional Distress,*
5. *Count V Consortium.*

They were going to file the complaint the next morning in the Circuit Court, Fourth Judicial Circuit, in and for Duval County, Florida.

Also in the complaint, they said:

Not only did the Defendants fail to provide adequate and operational ventilation, but also, to further reduce costs, the Defendants, even on occasion when the toxic fume stacks were fully operational, simply turned them off.

After the meeting, we all stood around in the lobby talking with several of the paralegals and staff about the case. I had a good feeling that we had a good firm representing us who had been there and done that type of case before.

The terms of agreement were that the law firm would receive thirty-three and one third percent of any monies recovered plus expenses, but this was standard in the business for personal injury cases.

Our entire group signed up except for Clinton who stayed with Henry Ferro at that time.

We all headed home feeling that we had good representation in both law firms.

As the case kept dragging on, I had to go to Ocala about every two months and sort through discovery evidence that was mostly useless information and garbage.

Oxy was just loading Dorothy down with garbage to make it look like they were complying with the discovery.

We also had to attend court ordered mediations that were a waste of time. Oxy raised their offers a little each time, but they were ridiculous offers.

We continued to have our support group meetings and tried to reassure each other that things were going to be all right.

It was 1999 and I had done everything I knew to do for this case and the people in it. By then, I already spent close to twenty thousand dollars on this case and my weight dropped to about 139 pounds from 176 when I first got sick.

My health was not good and seemed to be worsening. I was suffering from a progressive muscle disease and in a great deal of pain.

Then along with the painful muscles, I also experienced:
1. *heart arrhythmias,*
2. *Chronic Obstructive Pulmonary Disease (COPD),*
3. *emphysema,*
4. *osteoporosis,*
5. *osteoarthritis,*
6. *toxic brain syndrome,*
7. *migraine headaches with aura (migraine headaches are preceded by some sort of visual disturbance known as an aura),*
8. *swelling feet and joints,*
9. *confusion, and memory loss.*

Somehow, I still managed to work the phones calling experts on fluoride exposures and searching the internet for more information that might help with the case.

I would send or communicate all my findings to Dorothy Sims for the workers comp case and to Boyer's firm for the personal injury case.

I spent the rest of 1999 doing what I could to help the lawsuit move forward, and the people involved keep their spirits up. My phone bill was usually around three hundred per month mainly talking with the attorneys, fellow plaintiffs, and experts around the country.

September 21, 1998

Re : Mr. Gary Pittman

To Whom it May Concern :

This letter is written by a former employee of Occidental Chemical Company at it's Florida operations, in White Springs, Fl. from Dec. 30, 1974 - April 1, 1993

Having several Supervisors during my employment for this length of time during my 18 years and three months work, I David L. Cason of Route 3, Box 17, Madison, Fl. , did observe their several Supervisors and their duties for the company and also for the employees assigned to them.

One such supervisor I took for observance was Mr. Gary Pittman, of Jasper, Fl. This person had all the qualifications for a leader of seven people of his immediate shift workers, in addition to a Maintinance crew, an electrican crew, plus truck drivers delivering supplies, 3 or 4 people on shipping dept. to load and unload freight cars to and from the Jacksonville terminal for liquid phosphate acid and also granulated phosphate for shipment to the overseas markets. (Russa for example, a 20 years contract).

Mr. Pittman was always pleasant to work for and always kept SAFTY RULES and work habits, a TOP PRIORITY. In short, got the work done in a SAFE and TEAM WORK MANNER for the company and at the same time avoid accidents on and off the job for a profit to the company and job security for the employees. , as there was dangerous equipment being used and a hazardous work enviroment involving acid fumes and solvents of several sorts, involved in the process of making the finished product of phosphate acid, sulfric acid, and a very toxic acid.

On one occasion I recall was that Mr. Pittman was unable to work in May of 1993,thus taking Medical leave of absence, which was a handicap to him in order for him to support him and his family.

Despite efforts for employees to wear proper safty gear to avoid acid fumes and all safty precautions obeyed as the company stressed to their employees on safty, I recall one instance of neglect in 1987 as a fume scrubber was dismanteled and out of operation until sometime in 1991. This method of operations is to remove and neutralize fumes being pulled this scrubber system by a water sprinkler of spray nozzles inside the scrubber, discharging the exhaust back to the enviroment, by discharge fans. This piece of equipment (stock # 1350-A) being out of operations this long, was brought to the attention of persons in the chain of command including shift supervisor,day supervisor, complex managers and was known by employees that someone had neglected to have it as a necessity to operations of a safe work place.

I now wish for Mr. Pittman to be compensated for his disability through the company and insurance coverage on his behalf.

Sincerely,

David L. Cason
Route 5, Box 6325
Madison, Fl. 32340

Dated
Sept 21st 1998

August 25, 1998

To Whom It May Concern:

I have known Gary Pittman most of my life and worked with and around him for several years at Occidental Chemical Corporation in White Springs, Florida. Gary was a hard and relentless worker.

I worked as a dryer operator at Suwanee River Mine, an operator and shift supervisor at Pollyphos, a shift supervisor at T.S.P. and D.A.P. Granulation plant, and a general services superintendent at Swift Creek Chemical plant. Employees working in the chemical plants had to work in acid fumes for hours at a time whenever they were cleaning tanks and just working in the plants while performing their normal job duties. In addition to the fumes that the employees were exposed to in the plants, there was also the air from the stacks which was dirty.

Stack tests were performed, but they were a joke. We were told when a test would be performed and were prepared for it. For example, at Pollyphos, recycle feed that had already been deflorinated but was not down to a 0.18% level was brought back to the reactors in the early morning hours on the day of a test. That way, when the test was started later in the day, only green feed would be used. The two reactors, each with 50 ton capacity beds, would be contaminated with deflorinated feed with a 6 to 7 hour retention time at a rate of 7 tons per hour. The stack test would be complete before the green feed completely filled the beds again. Thus, the stacks appeared clean for the test. At one time, the cooler stack was not being checked and was loaded with fluorine because it did not have a scrubber.

In addition, at Granulation, the air was so dusty you could not leave the control room most of the time without a respirator. Cars in the parking lot would be covered with dust; dust that contained high levels of phosphoric acid and sulfuric acid. This dust would "eat" the windshields and paint on the cars. People breathed this air all the time. During a stack test, the employees worked overtime cleaning screens and sprays until the test was complete.

At the Super Acid plant, it rained acid so heavily from the stack that most of the time it would "eat" holes in the secretaries' stockings and panty hose between the parking lot and the office.

These are just some of the conditions that Gary had to work in during the time he worked at Occidental.

Sincerely,

Bobby Greene
Smithville, Texas
Occidental 1964 - 1980

29

Advanced

Metabolic Imaging / North Dallas, Inc.

12200 Preston Road   (214)490-0536   Dallas, Texas 75230

Theodore R. Simon, M.D   *Telecopier*   *David C. Hickey, M.D.*
(214) 528-2482 ■■■ (214)490-9727 ■■■ (214) 661-7679

April 24, 1996

William Rea, M.D.
8345 Walnut Hill Ln., Ste. 205
Dallas, TX 75231

RE: Pittman, Gary
     BRAIN SPECT SCAN, FLOW AND FUNCTION
     COMPLEX COMPUTER ANALYSIS

Dear Dr. Rea:

Mr. Pittman is undergoing evaluation for toxic encephalopathy, possibly from heavy metals with complaint of a daily headache, short term memory loss, and balance difficulties. He scored a 30 out of a possible 30 on the mini-mental examination. He was injected with 26.6 millicuries of technetium-99m HMPaO which is 90.3% bound. Single photon emission computed tomography was performed during both the flow and functional phases. Both sets of SPECT data were computer processed, filtered, and back-projected onto three planes orthogonal to the canthomeatal plane. Planar images were also obtained to evaluate attenuation and to provide quantitation. There was no patient motion during the exam.

There is a mild decoupling or dissociation between the early and late phases. There is a large area involving portions of the frontal, parietal, and left temporal regions with reduced early and late phase activity raising a concern for the possibility of a vascular stenosis in the left internal carotid artery/MCA distribution. A carotid Doppler and transcranial Doppler study may be a consideration in this patient.

Additional findings in this patient include a hot focus or activation area in the right frontal parietal region. The temporal lobes are asymmetric. Correlation for what appears to be an elevation in early phase activity and the delayed functional activity in the right temporal lobe compared to the left is suggested. Overall, the pattern is consistent with the findings in other patients with a history of neurotoxic exposure. The severity of the findings would be graded in the mild to moderate range. Included in the patient's history was a question of some liver problems perhaps secondary to heavy metal toxicity. Consideration of Ultrafast CT for measuring the patient's liver density is suggested. Additionally, in view of the possibility of atherosclerotic disease in the carotid region, one might wish to consider performing an Ultrafast CT for detection of coronary artery calcium and at least consider whether any dynamic breathing CT studies may be useful in this patient who may have COPD.

Thank you for allowing us to consult on Mr. Pittman for you.

Sincerely,

David C. Hickey, M.D.
jl
   4/25/96

Environmental Health Center — Dallas

8345 Walnut Hill Lane, Suite 220, Dallas, Texas 75231 • Telephone – (214) 368-4132 – FAX: (214) 691-84
e-mail: inform@ehcd.com • Worldwide Web site: www.ehcd.com

August 28, 1996

William J. Rea, M.D.
F.A.C.S., F.A.A.E.M.,
F.A.C.N., F.A.C.P.M.,
F.A.C.A., F.R.S.M.
Board Certified in
Thoracic and Cardiovascular Surgery
Abdominal and General Surgery
Environmental Medicine

Alfred R. Johnson, D.O.
F.A.A.E.M., D.I.B.E.M.
Internal Medicine
Allergy and Environmental Medicine

Gerald H. Ross, M.D., C.C.F.P.
I.B.E.M., D.A.B.E.M., F.A.A.E.M.,
F.R.S.M
Family Practice
Environmental Medicine

Ervin J. Fenyves, Ph.D.
Environmental Science

Bertie Griffiths, Ph.D.
Immunology
Microbiology

Carolyn Gorman, M.A.
Health Education

Teena Petree, B.S.P.T.
Physical Therapy

Judith J. Pruzzo - Hawkins
R.Ph., C.C.H
Homeopathy

Colette Bureau, L.A.C. Dipl. Ac.,
L.Ac., (NCCA)
Accupuncture

Lynn Kogenti, M.S., R.D., L.D.
Nutrition

Zenne Jones, R.D., L.D.
Nutrition

Rick A. Sellers. M.B.A.
Health Services

To Whom It May Concern:

RE: Gary Pittman

Mr. Pittman was first seen on April 22, 1996, with the chief complaints of muscle weakness, fatigue, irregular heartbeat, incoordination, swelling of the feet, ankles and joint, neck pain and weakness, headaches, dizziness, shortness of breath and coughing.

The physical exam revealed a blood pressure of 150/80, pulse 108, height 6, weight 172, respiration 22 and temperature of 97.4. The patient has lost most of his teeth. His nasal passages were extremely swollen and erythematous. On neurological examination he revealed a positive romberg and short term memory loss. He had a waddling wide gait and his feet were cyanotic.

He had a Volatile Aliphatic panel which showed an elevated level of n-Hexane. The Volatile Panel showed an elevated level of Benzene, 1, 1, 1, Trichloroethane.

He had a brain SPECT scan which showed a pattern which is consistent with neurotoxic exposure.

Mr. Pittman had a hair analysis which showed elevated levels of calcium, zinc, iron, manganese, vanadium and selenium. He had low levels of chromium, boron, lithium and sulfur.

It is my medical opinion that Mr. Pittman is totally disabled and it is undetermined when he will be able to return to work.

If you have any questions concerning this, please do not hesitate to contact my office.

Sincerely,

William J. Rea, M.D.

WJR:mis

40

Department of
Environmental Protection

Northeast District
7825 Baymeadows Way, Suite B200
Jacksonville, Florida 32216-7591

January 22, 1996

Lawton Chiles
Governor

Virginia B. Wetherell
Secretary

Mr. Gary Pittman
Route 1, Box 85A
Jennings, Florida 32053

Dear Mr. Pittman:

> Hamilton County AP
> White Springs Agricultural /
> Occidental Chemical
> Enforcement Cases

In responce to your phone call here is a list of the enforcement
cases in the Northeast District for White Springs Agricultural /
Occidental in air:

Identification	Problem	Fine
8/30/95	Fail Stack Test C & D SPA	$6,000
7/20/94	Fail Stack Test C Phos Acid	12,500
OGC91-079		200
90-1626		100
86-1356	Start-up 4 acid plants,agricultural damage	Paid state to install 2 ambient monitors
79-72	Misrepresenting environmental data	a) Funding position monitor OXY activities
		b) $575,000

I hope this information is helpful.

Sincerely,

Morton Benjamin

Morton Benjamin

32

"Protect, Conserve and Manage Florida's Environment and Natural Resources"

Printed on recycled paper

104

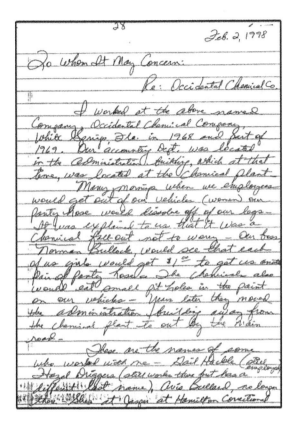

Feb 2, 1998

To whom it may concern,

Re: Occidental Chemical Co.

I worked at the above named Company, Occidental Chemical Company, White springs, Fla. In 1968 and part of 1969. Our accounting Dept was located in the Administration building, which at that time, was located at the chemical plant.

Many mornings when we employees would get out of our vehicles (women) our panty hose would dissolve off our legs. It was explained to us that it was a chemical fall-out not to worry – Our boss Norman Bullock would see that each of us girls would get $1.00 to get another pair of panty hose. The chemicals would also eat small pit holes in the paint on our vehicles – years later they moved the administration building away from the chemical plant to out by the main road…

Appellee primarily relies on *Cunningham v. Anchor Hocking Corp.*, 558 So.2d 93 (Fla. 1st DCA) *rev. denied*, 574 So.2d 139 (Fla.1990), and *Connelly v. Arrow Air, Inc.*, 568 So.2d 448 (Fla. 3d DCA 1990), *rev. denied*, 581 So.2d 1307 (Fla.1991), to support its argument for allowing a third-party claim against an employer despite an employer's entitlement to workers' compensation immunity. In *Cunningham*, the plaintiff had alleged an intentional tort based on the following facts: The employer had deliberately diverted a smoke stack so that dangerous fumes would flow into rather than outside of the building; the employer periodically turned off the ventilation system; the employer had removed the manufacturer's warning labels on toxic substances; the employer misrepresented the toxic nature of the substances involved; the employer misrepresented the effectiveness of safety equipment and the danger involved; the employer provided inadequate safety equipment. In *Connelly*, which involved an airplane crash, the employer had misrepresented the

Memos Indicate Company
Authorized Illegal Pollution

(c) New York Times

NEW YORK — The Hooker Chemical and Plastics Corp. was convicted in 1978 of polluting Florida's air with fluoride, but previously unpublished documents show that the company's phosphorus plant in White Springs had far more violations than the authorities suspected and that the company's top echelon knew and approved of the local manager's violating the plant's emissions permit.

According to the memorandums, plant officers also shut down or changed the operation of their smokestacks and spillways when inspectors visited them or when emissions tests for permit compliance were run, breaking state and federal laws.

Hooker received publicity last year when chemicals it had dumped in Niagara Falls' Love Canal neighborhood leaked into backyards and basements, forcing the evacuation of 239 homes.

Documents dealing with the White Springs operation showed that, while point rebuttal of specific issues raised by the press which are based on documents furnished by the company to governmental agencies"

Tabris said the company voluntarily reported some violations to authorities in April 1978. Employees were granted immunity from prosecution, he said, and the company pleaded no contest, subjecting itself to a conviction, so it considered the case closed.

He also said the company's plant was operating in compliance with regulations and no damage had resulted from the known violations

Other Hooker plants and landfills release chemicals more dangerous than fluoride, and Hooker has admitted keeping quiet about accidentally poisoning groundwater and drinking wells at its plants in Niagara Falls, Montague, Mich., and Lathrop, Calif. But this is the first evidence that the company's top management authorized violations of pollution laws

The memorandums were released from company files last fall when the Mead Paper Corp. sued the Occidental Petroleum Corp., Hooker's parent company, which was trying to buy a controlling share in Mead. The documents have been in the hands of the Florida Department of Environmental Regulation, the Environmental Protection Agency (EPA), the Securities and Exchange Commission and House and Senate subcommittees for several months

The Justice Department and EPA are investigating the company's dumping practices and water pollution at its plants across the nation. Under federal law, the penalty for giving false information to a U.S. agency is up to five years in prison and a $10,000 fine

Though less dangerous than some pollutants, fluoride is harmful in amounts vastly larger than those that go into water systems.

The Hooker plant's releases of fluoride and phosphate were into the Suwannee River, the only major river in the Southeastern flood plain that is relatively unspoiled.

Chapter Sixteen

When we filed the lawsuit in Jacksonville, and Oxy hired Holland and Knight to represent them. Holland and Knight is an international law firm with more than 1000 lawyers in 17 U.S. cities. They were an established legal representative for most of the phosphate companies and citrus groves of Polk County, Florida. They specialized in defending corporations against cases like ours, and were willing to go to any lengths to win.

We were up against some real merciless, legal sharks. At that time, it was one of those eat or be eaten games.

Oxy hired one of the heaviest hitting law firms in the world to represent them. However, it was a good sign to me because I had a feeling that Oxy was on the verge of making a reasonable settlement.

The case was growing and gaining momentum everyday.

Tyree put out a press release when he filed the case, and in it he said, "If you fire a gun into a crowd you're probably going to hit someone."

He was referring to the chemicals. If enough people are exposed then you are probably going to make some sick.

In January of 2000, I got a telephone call to go to a mediation session at Dorothy's office in Gainesville. I arrived and waited for mediation to begin.

I went in and there was an attorney present that I never met before. We talked for a bit, and he made an offer for settlement. I refused it without Dorothy present. Then he asked, "How much would it take to make you go away?"

I thought about it a few minutes and wrote a number down on the sheet of paper.

He looked at the paper and said, "I can make that happen if you settle both the workers comp suit and the personal injury case."

I told him I needed to think about it. He told me the offer was on the table.

I went home and thought about the offer. Later, I called Dorothy and she thought that it was a reasonable offer and really couldn't believe it.

I wanted to talk with Tyree about the offer so I called his office to discuss the offer.

I thought that the personal injury lawsuit was worrying Oxy now. It was growing, and starting to get out of hand, and they wanted to end it.

I talked with Tyree and told him about the offer. He told me to take the offer because it was a sure thing. He said we could go forward and lose, and then I would get nothing.

I had a wife and four children to think about, and our finances dwindled during those last seven years of battling Oxy.

There was a standard nondisclosure agreement with the settlement offer, so I couldn't tell anyone about the amount I would receive.

However, I found out later that they also offered several other plaintiffs settlements. Most of the people I spoke to weren't happy with their offers and told me what they were.

After talking with my wife, I decided to take the offer.

Tyree called a meeting of all the plaintiffs in the personal injury lawsuit.

We all sat down and discussed the offers made at the mediation. I did not discuss mine because of the nondisclosure agreement.

Tyree already knew the amount of my offer. He advised all of the plaintiffs that it would be in their best interests to take their offers, but most of them told him they would not.

He then explained that if they didn't take the settlement offers they needed to seek new council because he was going to withdraw from the case.

We all left and went home.

Our support group got together and we discussed the case.

One other person besides me decided to accept the settlement, and that was Billy Baldwin. Billy went through chemotherapy for leukemia and was in remission. Billy, like me was just tired and wanted to try to get back to some sort of normal life.

The other members of the group vowed to fight on and seek a new counsel for the personal injury case that I started.

We had been through a lot together, and I wished them well. But l knew that there would be hard feelings toward me from some people because they felt, I abandoned them and gave up the fight.

However, at the very beginning, we discussed the fact that if anyone received an offer they could live with, he or she should take it.

Essentially, that's why we didn't go for a class action lawsuit where the settlement is equally divided among the plaintiffs. Everybody agreed on that stance from the onset.

I was sure the main reason Oxy wanted to settle with me was because I had been the leader and spokesperson for the group since the case began.

They figured if that I were gone, the lawsuit would fall apart.

It took a good deal of time for the lawyers to workout the details on my settlement because of some stipulations I wanted to add.

In the meantime, Tyree withdrew from the case, and Jesse Nash and some of the others hired a new lawyer to take over the lawsuit.

Miguel A. Mendez Jr. P.A. from West Palm Beach, Florida began representing Jesse Nash and some of the others.

Jesse called me one evening and wanted me to attend a meeting at the Holiday Inn in Lake City, Florida. Miguel also wanted me to attend.

Jesse and the group wanted me to hear what Miguel had to say before I signed my settlement papers.

When the meeting day came, Gloria and I headed off to Lake City.

Miguel and his staff were signing up new plaintiffs when I arrived.

I had a soda pop with Jesse before the meeting, and later listened to what Miguel had to say.

During that last seven years, I talked to a lot lawyers, and I heard the same pitch on more than several occasions. I didn't sign on with Miguel, but I promised to think about it.

Gloria and I talked about it in detail. I had a concrete offer on the table and Tyree and Dorothy advised me to take it.

I was ill, had the futures of Gloria and my four children to think about, and my health wasn't improving.

During those previous seven years, I helped bury several of the plaintiffs who were also my friends, and well knew I might only have a short time left. I wanted to make sure that my wife and kids had enough money to keep them going if I died the next day.

I also just didn't think Miguel could get me a better offer. I also knew that if I didn't take the settlement, I might wind up with nothing.

I liked Miguel and thought he was a competent attorney, but I was tired and sick, and I decided to settle rather than chance walking away with nothing.

I called Jesse and told him my decision, and that it was best for my family. Jesse was always a first class type of fellow and wished me the best. I wished him good luck with the case.

In a couple of weeks, my settlement was ready. I traveled to Gainesville, Florida and signed the settlement papers in the judge's chambers. My fight had lasted seven years and I was very tired and ill.

As time went on, I kept up with the lawsuit. Miguel had about 300-400 plaintiffs now onboard according to one newspaper articles.

I heard through the grapevine that some of the plaintiffs were upset with me because I settled. They thought I should have fought on, but I had a feeling in my gut that I did the right thing.

After going through seven years of hell, I felt I had to do something to help the other people. I learned a lot about the synergistic effects of fluorides.

I worked in the phosphoric acid business for many years and knew that the byproduct fluorosilicic acid was some bad stuff. I also knew that industry was selling this stuff to cities to add to the drinking water saying it was good for children because it helped to prevent tooth decay.

The reality is that they've never did any health and study studies using the fluorosilicic acid from the pollution scrubbers. All the studies were done with a pharmaceutical grade sodium fluoride and distilled water, which is very different from the fluoride pollution captured in the scrubbers.

The truth of the matter is that the US Government or anyone else that promotes drinking water fluoridation and says it safe based on studies done with a different product with different toxicological properties is just not telling the truth or just don't know what their talking about.

There are many good articles and books written by good scientists about the subject, and they most say the fluosilicic acid isn't good for our health.

I wrote a letter addressed to Congress describing the fluosilicic acid and the dangers involved in adding it to our drinking water. I asked that they stop this foolish practice and enact stricter laws regarding phosphoric acid production.[11]

I am not a scientist but do know I do not want this witch's brew in my water and will not knowingly drink it.

Chapter Seventeen

It was toward the end of 2000, I received a subpoena to appear in Lake City for a deposition. It was an order to compel a discovery deposition of Gary Pittman, and I was to appear for Miguel Mendez Jr., P.A.

The subpoena included a production list of any files, pictures, and documents that I had in my possession regarding Gary Owen Pittman vs. Occidental Chemical Company.

The deposition was going to be for Jesse Nash and the other plaintiffs.

I arrived in Lake City with a large suitcase of documents and work product from my lawsuit. My settlement papers stated that I could not talk to anyone that worked for Oxy unless subpoenaed.

Present at the deposition was Miguel Mendez, Jesse Nash, and Clinton Vann along with Oxy's lawyers.

I was representing myself. I asked Miguel if we could call the judge to make sure this subpoena overruled my settlement agreement. He agreed and we called the judge to make sure it was alright if I gave the deposition and answered their all the questions.

After much confusion, the ball fell in my court to make the decision whether or not to answer the questions. The judge was not very helpful and said he couldn't advise me. They had a subpoena so I told them to go ahead and start the deposition. Of course, Oxy's lawyers objected and advised me not to talk.

I was caught between the rock and the hard place, and I finally told Miguel to start the deposition.

Miguel started the deposition in the usual way, and asked me to state my name and address and where I worked.

---

* See Appendix.

Then Miguel and his assistants began searching through the suitcase and briefcase full of documents that they requested in the subpoena, and began questioning me about them.

We slowly went through documents, letters, and my research. The assistants would mark and tag each piece as he questioned me. Then they asked me to initial each document when I answered a question about it. We stopped only for lunch.

The deposition continued into late afternoon and ended with about half of my files still left for examination. They said we would continue deposition at a later date and that I should keep in touch with them.

I left and drove home.

Later that week, Jesse called and we talked some. Jesse had a sore on his tongue and was going to have it surgically removed.

About a week later, he called and told me it was cancer, but the surgeon said they got it all.

As time went on, I didn't hear from anyone involved in the lawsuit.

Once in awhile I would read an article in the newspaper about the case, but no one ever called and asked me to finish my deposition.

I learned through a mutual friend that Jesse was worse and his cancer was back. I called Jesse to talk and see how he was doing. He told me that he was done, and he didn't have long to live. A CAT scan showed the cancer had spread to all of his organs.

I told Jesse that I would pray for him and wished I could help him. I wanted see Jesse before he died. We went through a lot together, and I wanted to say my goodbye to my old friend in person. It was the least I could do for Jesse, and most I definitely owed him that for his loyalty and friendship.

I contacted Clinton, and we drove down to Lake City to see Jesse one last time.

Jesse was in terrible condition. He lost a lot of weight, and he didn't look like he had long to go. He weighed about two hundred pounds when we worked together, and was very athletic. Jesse was a diver and loved looking for ancient Indian artifacts in the Suwannee River. His artifact collection was his pride and joy.

At the plant, he was one of the top men on the company fire brigade, and Israeli firemen invited him to work at one of their departments for several months on some type of exchange program.

Before he went to work at Oxy, he was a Highway Patrol Trooper in Hillsboro County, Florida.

George Glasser and Jesse were tight. They had a common interest - they both loved prehistoric Florida archeology and liked to go artifact hunting. They even traded their artifacts with each other. They genuinely liked one another and communicated on a regular bases.

Jesse was also a good family man and a person who liked to be friends with everyone – just a good, likeable fellow to know.

Seeing him in that condition was heartbreaking.

Jesse and I visited. He was chipper despite his health. I started to leave and told him goodbye. The last words he said to me were, "Bye Buddy."

I went home very sad and knew Jesse was close to death. He gave me a framed poem when we were in the war with Oxy, and it still hangs above my desk in my office today. There is also a picture of me, Clinton and Jesse. It gives me inspiration. The poem was as follows:

"It is not the critic who counts; not the man who points out how the strong man stumbles, or where the doer of deeds could have done them better. The credit belongs to the man who is actually in the arena, whose face is marred by dust and sweat and blood, who strives valiantly; who errs and comes short again and again; because there is not effort without error and shortcomings; but who does actually strive to do the deed; who knows the great enthusiasm, the great devotion, who spends himself in a worthy cause, who at the best knows in the end the triumph of high achievement and who at the worst, if he fails, at least he fails while daring greatly. So that his place shall never be with those cold and timid souls who know neither victory nor defeat."

Clinton Vann called me about two weeks after our visit with Jesse. He told me Jesse died that evening. I was very sad and my mind was wondering back over the last thirty years. I could see all the faces of the people I had worked with. We were all young, strong, full of enthusiasm, and laughing while doing our jobs.

Around 2003 I stopped hearing or reading anything about the lawsuit. However, I heard that it was at a standstill. Rumor was that the case became too expensive for the plaintiffs' law firm to pursue.

I purchased a larger home for my family in a peaceful neighborhood near Jennings named Timberlake.

I still suffer from migraine headaches, autoimmune muscle disease, COPD, emphysema, osteoarthritis, neuropathy, toxic encephalopathy and osteoporosis. Last year, my doctor diagnosed me with early stage dementia.

On top of that, they say I have polymycemia. My bones are producing too many blood cells and I have to let one pint of blood a month.

I don't know what fate awaits me, but I do know that I had the pleasure of working with some the finest, courageous people I've ever known.

I think of all of them often and dream about our fight. Was it all worth it? Yes - because in my heart, I know that I gave it my very best, and win or lose, that is all a person can do.

THE END

Conclusion

From experience, I would advise anyone working in an industrial environment and exposed to toxic chemicals no matter how small the dose to keep a daily journal of the workday. Document any exposures, the date and time.

Always ask for a MSDS and make sure you have proper personal protective equipment, if not talk with your supervisor and ask him to obtain it for you.

If you see a hazard report it, and if it goes unresolved, then report it to the proper authorities such as OSHA or the EPA.

If you are exposed for many years, become ill, and need to file for benefits, seek a doctor who will listen to your problems and take your work history into account.

If he doesn't then find another doctor because he can not treat you without understanding your exposures.

If you find you need an attorney, file your case promptly because there is a statute of limitations on your case. The statute of limitations is usually two years from the time you knew you were exposed to the toxic substances and became ill.

You also need to find an attorney that is experienced in chemical exposure toxic tort cases. Almost any personal injury lawyer will take your case, but all of them have the experience to represent you properly.

Most importantly, you must find an attorney that is hungry to win your case. Chemical exposure is very hard to prove but determination and relentlessness is the key if you are going to win your case.

Going into a case, you need to know as much as possible about the chemicals you worked with and be prepared to do a lot of your own research.

Lastly, the more media attention you can draw to your case the better because it puts pressure on the company to settle. Write your story down on paper so you can give it to a reporter, and don't be afraid to start contacting journalists and editors about your case.

Appendix

OSHA violations 1973-1991

Sulfuric Acid Emissions

Occidental Exposures: Gary's Story

Earth Island Journal - Winter/Spring 1999 *by George C. Glasser*

Fluoride and the Phosphate Connection

Earth Island Journal Special Feature

Fluorides and the Environment

Summer/Fall 1997 by George C. Glasser

Pittman Letter to Senate/Congress

Excerpts from the article *Death in the Air* George Glasser (1999): Wives' Comments

Occidental Safety Violations – 1973-1996

 U.S. Department of Labor

Occupational Safety and Health Administration

Ribault Building, Suite 227
1851 Executive Center Drive
Jacksonville, Florida 32207
COMM: (904) 232-2895
FAX : (904) 232-1294
Reply to the Attention of: Area Director

January 31, 1996

Gary O. Pittman
Route 1, Box 85-A
Jennings, FL 32053

    RE: Freedom of Information Act (FOIA) request No. 96-017 for
         information about any OSHA citations and penalties issued
         to "Occidental Chemical Corp.", White Springs, Florida,
         from 1965 to 1995.

Dear Mr. Pittman:

This is in response to your FOIA request dated January 25, 1996,
and referenced above.

As you and I discussed over the telephone on January 26th, I
reviewed our records and discovered that "Occidental Chemical" at
White Springs, had been inspected twenty times by OSHA; starting in
1973 to 1991.

You indicated to me that a computer report showing the dates of
inspections and if any citations and penalties were issued, would
satisfy your request. I have attached a SCAN computer report
titled: "OSHA History of 'Occidental Chemical', White Springs, FL
From January 1973 to January 1996."

This report shows the twenty inspections conducted, when they were
conducted, what the results were in terms of citations and
penalties, and the reason for the inspection, plus additional
information.

I am considering this response as fully honoring your request.
Once your receive this report, and have any questions, please do
not hesitate to contact me.

If I may be of further assistance with this matter, please contact
me and reference FOIA No. 96-017. Your interest in occupational
safety and health is appreciated.

Sincerely,

James D. Borders
Area Director

Attachment

33

DOL-OSHA-OMDS U. S. D E P A R T M E N T O F L A B O R 960

(RSCHSCAN) OCCUPATIONAL SAFETY AND HEALTH ADMINISTRATION

IMIS REPORT
KEEP THIS PAGE WITH THIS REPORT.
IT CONTAINS IMPORTANT INFORMATION ABOUT
THE WAY CASES WERE SELECTED

TYPE OF REPORT: SCAN

USER SELECTION NAME: FOIA6017

DATE OF REPORT: 960130

REQUESTOR: OSH336

REPORT TITLE: OSHA HISTORY OF "OCCIDENTAL CHEMICAL", WHITE SPRINGS, FL FROM JANUARY 1973 TO JANUARY 1996

FOOT NOTE: FOIA 96-017

************************** SELECTION CRITERIA **************************

OPEN DATE FROM 730101 TO 960129

REPORT ID: 04197

FEDERAL AND 18(B) STATE

SORT ORDER: OPEN-DATE

ABSTRACT OPTION: N

STATE SPECIFIED: FL
CITIES: 3220
COUNTIES: 047

ESTABLISHMENT STRING(S):/OCCIDENTAL CHEMICAL/

ACCIDENT FLAG: Y

```
ESTABLISHMENT INSPECTED       REPORT ID ACTIVITY# CSHO     SIC1/SIC2
ADDRESS                       OPEN DATE INSP TYPE CATEGORY %REMITTED  EMPESTAB
CITY             STATE ZIP    CLOSECONF OPT REPT# SCOPE    OWNERSHIP  EMPINSP    LWDI
COUNTY (NAME/CODE)            CASE CLSD PREV ACT  UNION    CLASS      EMPCNTRL
                             RELTD ACT
```

STANDARD	CITATION TYP	GR RE IDENT VC	AST ISSUANCE DATE	ABATE DATE	CMP CDE	INITIAL PENALTY	CURRENT PENALTY	INITIAL F-T-A PENALTY	CURRENT F-T-A PENALTY	C SETTLM-T N DISPOS-N T /FINORDT	HAZD SUBS CODE

```
*******************************
OCCIDENTAL CHEMICAL CO DIV   0419700   013668967 G3762-1  2870
PO BOX 300                   2/09/73   UN-CMPLNT HEALTH    205        347
White Springs    FL 32096    2/09/73   151002173 COMPREH              347
Hamilton         047         3/10/84   (NONE)    NONUNION             347  (PENALTIES PAID)

         1910.252 E02  III      0 01001      3/01/73  4/17/73 X    45      45      0     0
         1910.095 B01           0 01002   C  3/01/73  4/17/73 X     0       0      0     0      8110
         1910.095 A             0 01003      3/01/73  3/05/73 X    30      30      0     0
         1910.111 B13           0 01004      3/01/73  4/17/73 X    55      55      0     0
         1910.215 A04           0 01005      3/01/73  3/05/73 X    40      40      0     0
         1910.132 A             0 01006      3/01/73  3/05/73 X    35      35      0     0
         1910.132 A             0 01007      3/01/73  3/05/73 X     0       0      0     0
                                         TOTAL PENALTIES   205     205      0     0
*******************************
OCCIDENTAL CHEMICAL CO DIV   0419700   013669692 G3762-1  2870
PO BOX 300                   11/12/74  UN-CMPLNT SAFETY     0        1013
White Springs    FL 32096    11/12/74  151008600 PARTIAL              18
Hamilton         047         3/10/84   (NONE)    NONUNION            1013
*******************************
OCCIDENTAL CHEMICAL CO-SUWANNE 0419700 013735295 S2776-C  2819
SR 137                       7/21/78   PR-PLANND SAFETY     0        1200
White Springs    FL 32096    7/27/78   151051200 PARTIAL             553
Hamilton         047         8/24/78   (NONE)    UNION    SPG-MFG   1200

         1926.450 A01           0 01001      8/15/78  8/15/78 X     0       0      0     0
*******************************
OCCIDENTAL CHEMICAL CO-SUWANNE 0419700 013660097 E0366-C  2819
SR 137                       10/26/78  UN-CMPLNT SAFETY     0        1200
White Springs    FL 32096    10/31/78  151019400 PARTIAL             20
Hamilton         047         11/20/78  (NONE)    UNION              1200
                             C320901945

         1910.180 C02           0 01001     11/08/78 11/11/78 X     0       0      0     0
         1910.180 I05   I       0 01002     11/08/78 11/11/78 X     0       0      0     0
```

```
ESTABLISHMENT INSPECTED      REPORT ID ACTIVITY# CSHO      SIC1/SIC2
ADDRESS                      OPEN DATE INSP TYPE CATEGORY $REMITTED  EMPESTAB
CITY            STATE ZIP    CLOSECONF OPT REPT# SCOPE     OWNERSHIP  EMPINSP    LWDI
COUNTY (NAME/CODE)           CASE CLSD PREV ACT  UNION     CLASS      EMPCNTRL
                             RELTD ACT
```

STANDARD	CITATION TYP	GR RE IDENT VC	ABT ISSUANCE ABATE CMP DATE DATE CDE	INITIAL PENALTY	CURRENT PENALTY	INITIAL F-T-A PENALTY	CURRENT F-T-A PENALTY	C SETTLM-T HAZD N DISPOS-N SUBS T /FINORDT CODE

```
*********************************
OCCIDENTAL CHEMICAL CO DIV   0419700   013622436 B6973-C 2819
PO BOX 300                   4/27/79   UN-FATCAT SAFETY      560        660
White Springs    FL 32096    5/11/79   151006900 PARTIAL                 6
Hamilton         047         6/15/79   (NONE)    UNION                 660  (PENALTIES PAID)
                             A350073870
```

1910.252 D02	XIVB	S 01001A	A 5/23/79 5/26/79 X	560	560	0	0
1910.252 D03	II	S 01001B	A 5/23/79 5/26/79 X	0	0	0	0

```
                         ****   ACCIDENT DATA   ****

        VICTIM: 001                   AGE: 00    SEX:    OCCUP: Not reported
                DISPOSITION : HOSPITALIZED INJURY  EVENT-TYPE : STRUCK BY
                INJ NATURE  : CUT/LACERATION        ENVIR FACTOR: FLYING OBJECT ACTION
                INJ SOURCE  : DUST/PARTICLES/CHIPS  HUMAN FACTOR: MISJUDGMENT, HAZ. SITUATION
                PART-OF-BODY: FACE                  HAZ SUBSTNCE: HYDROGEN

        VICTIM: 002                   AGE: 00    SEX:    OCCUP: Not reported
                DISPOSITION : FATALITY             EVENT-TYPE : STRUCK AGAINST
                INJ NATURE  : FRACTURE             ENVIR FACTOR: OVERPRESSURE/UNDERPRESSURE
                INJ SOURCE  : OTHER                HUMAN FACTOR: MISJUDGMENT, HAZ. SITUATION
                PART-OF-BODY: NECK                 HAZ SUBSTNCE: HYDROGEN
*********************************
OCCIDENTAL CHEMICAL CO DIV   0419700   013622444 B6973-C 2819
PO BOX 300                   6/05/79   UN-FOLLOW SAFETY       0         660
White Springs    FL 32096    6/05/79   151007000 PARTIAL                 6
Hamilton         047         3/10/84   (NONE)    UNION                 660
*********************************
OCCIDENTAL CHEMICAL CO DIVISIO 0419700 013698667 K4370-C 2874
SUWANNEE RIVER COMPLEX       4/29/80   UN-FATCAT SAFETY     1800       2000
White Springs    FL 32096    5/13/80   151009500 PARTIAL                50
Hamilton         047         8/19/80   (NONE)    UNION                2000  (PENALTIES PAID)
                             A350074225
                             C320906100
```

5A.001		S 01001	6/27/80 6/30/80 X	720	720	0	0
1910.309 A	025045	S 01002	6/27/80 4/29/80 X	630	630	0	0
1910.219 D01		S 01003	6/27/80 6/30/80 X	450	450	0	0
1910.243 C03		O 02001	6/27/80 4/29/80 X	0	0	0	0
1910.023 A08		O 02002	6/27/80 5/06/80 X	0	0	0	0

```
ESTABLISHMENT INSPECTED      REPORT ID ACTIVITY# CSHO    SIC1/SIC2
ADDRESS                      OPEN DATE INSP TYPE CATEGORY $REMITTED EMPESTAB
CITY            STATE ZIP    CLOSECONF OPT REPT# SCOPE    OWNERSHIP EMPINSP   LWDI
COUNTY (NAME/CODE)           CASE CLSD PREV ACT  UNION    CLASS     EMPCNTRL
                             RELTD ACT
```

STANDARD	CITATION TYP	IDENT	GR RE VC	ISSUANCE DATE	ABATE DATE	ABT CMP CDE	INITIAL PENALTY	CURRENT PENALTY	INITIAL F-T-A PENALTY	CURRENT F-T-A PENALTY	C SETTLM-T HA2D N DISPOS-N SUBS T /FINORDT CODE
****************************										
OCCIDENTAL CHEMICAL CO DIVISIO 0419700 013698667				*** CONTINUED ***						
1910.106 D02	I	0 02003		6/27/80	6/30/80	X	0	0	0	0	
1910.180 I05	I	0 02004		6/27/80	6/30/80	X	0	0	0	0	
					TOTAL PENALTIES		1800	1800	0	0	

```
                         ****   ACCIDENT DATA   ****

        VICTIM: 001                AGE: 00    SEX:    OCCUP: Not reported
                DISPOSITION : HOSPITALIZED INJURY   EVENT-TYPE : OTHER
                INJ NATURE  : BURN/SCALD(HEAT)       ENVIR FACTOR: GAS/VAPOR/MIST/FUME/SMOKE/DUST
                INJ SOURCE  : FIRE/SMOKE             HUMAN FACTOR: OTHER
                PART-OF-BODY: MULTIPLE               HAZ SUBSTNCE: 1830 (NAME NOT IN TABLE)

        VICTIM: 002                AGE: 00    SEX:    OCCUP: Not reported
                DISPOSITION : HOSPITALIZED INJURY   EVENT-TYPE : OTHER
                INJ NATURE  : BURN/SCALD(HEAT)       ENVIR FACTOR: GAS/VAPOR/MIST/FUME/SMOKE/DUST
                INJ SOURCE  : FIRE/SMOKE             HUMAN FACTOR: OTHER
                PART-OF-BODY: MULTIPLE               HAZ SUBSTNCE: 1830 (NAME NOT IN TABLE)

        VICTIM: 003                AGE: 00    SEX:    OCCUP: Not reported
                DISPOSITION : HOSPITALIZED INJURY   EVENT-TYPE : OTHER
                INJ NATURE  : BURN/SCALD(HEAT)       ENVIR FACTOR: GAS/VAPOR/MIST/FUME/SMOKE/DUST
                INJ SOURCE  : FIRE/SMOKE             HUMAN FACTOR: OTHER
                PART-OF-BODY: MULTIPLE               HAZ SUBSTNCE: 1830 (NAME NOT IN TABLE)

        VICTIM: 004                AGE: 00    SEX:    OCCUP: Not reported
                DISPOSITION : HOSPITALIZED INJURY   EVENT-TYPE : OTHER
                INJ NATURE  : BURN/SCALD(HEAT)       ENVIR FACTOR: GAS/VAPOR/MIST/FUME/SMOKE/DUST
                INJ SOURCE  : FIRE/SMOKE             HUMAN FACTOR: OTHER
                PART-OF-BODY: MULTIPLE               HAZ SUBSTNCE: 1830 (NAME NOT IN TABLE)

        VICTIM: 005                AGE: 00    SEX:    OCCUP: Not reported
                DISPOSITION : HOSPITALIZED INJURY   EVENT-TYPE : OTHER
                INJ NATURE  : BURN/SCALD(HEAT)       ENVIR FACTOR: GAS/VAPOR/MIST/FUME/SMOKE/DUST
                INJ SOURCE  : FIRE/SMOKE             HUMAN FACTOR: OTHER
                PART-OF-BODY: MULTIPLE               HAZ SUBSTNCE: 1830 (NAME NOT IN TABLE)
```

```
ESTABLISHMENT INSPECTED        REPORT ID ACTIVITY# CSHO     SIC1/SIC2
ADDRESS                        OPEN DATE INSP TYPE CATEGORY $REMITTED  EMPESTAB
CITY            STATE ZIP  CLOSECONF OPT REPT# SCOPE     OWNERSHIP  EMPINSP   LWDI
COUNTY (NAME/CODE)             CASE CLSD PREV ACT  UNION      CLASS      EMPCNTRL
                               RELTD ACT
```

				GR			AST				INITIAL	CURRENT	C SETTLM-T HAZD
		CITATION	RE ISSUANCE	ABATE	CMP	INITIAL	CURRENT	F-T-A	F-T-A	N DISPOS-N SUBS
STANDARD		TYP IDENT	VC	DATE	DATE CDE	PENALTY	PENALTY	PENALTY	PENALTY	T /FINORDT CODE

```
*******************************
OCCIDENTAL CHEMICAL CO DIVISIO 0419700   013698667   *** CONTINUED ***

            VICTIM: 006              AGE: 00    SEX:    OCCUP: Not reported
                DISPOSITION : HOSPITALIZED INJURY   EVENT-TYPE : OTHER
                INJ NATURE  : BURN/SCALD(HEAT)       ENVIR FACTOR: GAS/VAPOR/MIST/FUME/SMOKE/DUST
                INJ SOURCE  : FIRE/SMOKE             HUMAN FACTOR: OTHER
                PART-OF-BODY: MULTIPLE               HAZ SUBSTNCE: 1830 (NAME NOT IN TABLE)

            VICTIM: 007              AGE: 00    SEX:    OCCUP: Not reported
                DISPOSITION : HOSPITALIZED INJURY   EVENT-TYPE : OTHER
                INJ NATURE  : BURN/SCALD(HEAT)       ENVIR FACTOR: GAS/VAPOR/MIST/FUME/SMOKE/DUST
                INJ SOURCE  : FIRE/SMOKE             HUMAN FACTOR: OTHER
                PART-OF-BODY: MULTIPLE               HAZ SUBSTNCE: 1830 (NAME NOT IN TABLE)

            VICTIM: 008              AGE: 00    SEX:    OCCUP: Not reported
                DISPOSITION : HOSPITALIZED INJURY   EVENT-TYPE : OTHER
                INJ NATURE  : BURN/SCALD(HEAT)       ENVIR FACTOR: GAS/VAPOR/MIST/FUME/SMOKE/DUST
                INJ SOURCE  : FIRE/SMOKE             HUMAN FACTOR: OTHER
                PART-OF-BODY: MULTIPLE               HAZ SUBSTNCE: 1830 (NAME NOT IN TABLE)

            VICTIM: 009              AGE: 00    SEX:    OCCUP: Not reported
                DISPOSITION : HOSPITALIZED INJURY   EVENT-TYPE : OTHER
                INJ NATURE  : BURN/SCALD(HEAT)       ENVIR FACTOR: GAS/VAPOR/MIST/FUME/SMOKE/DUST
                INJ SOURCE  : FIRE/SMOKE             HUMAN FACTOR: OTHER
                PART-OF-BODY: MULTIPLE               HAZ SUBSTNCE: 1830 (NAME NOT IN TABLE)

            VICTIM: 010              AGE: 00    SEX:    OCCUP: Not reported
                DISPOSITION : HOSPITALIZED INJURY   EVENT-TYPE : OTHER
                INJ NATURE  : BURN/SCALD(HEAT)       ENVIR FACTOR: GAS/VAPOR/MIST/FUME/SMOKE/DUST
                INJ SOURCE  : FIRE/SMOKE             HUMAN FACTOR: OTHER
                PART-OF-BODY: HAND(S)                HAZ SUBSTNCE: 1830 (NAME NOT IN TABLE)
*******************************
OCCIDENTAL CHEMICAL CO-SUWANNE 0419700   013608617 81655-I 2874
RT OFF US 41 ON C137 TO SIGN   5/28/80  UN-CMPLNT HEALTH       0        2100
White Springs        FL 32096  5/28/80  151015400 PARTIAL               1200
Hamilton             047       3/02/81  (NONE)    UNION                 2100
                                        C320906217

        1910.134 A03           O 01001A   8/12/80 8/15/80 N     0        0        0        0        9135
```

```
ESTABLISHMENT INSPECTED      REPORT ID ACTIVITY# CSNO    SIC1/SIC2
ADDRESS                      OPEN DATE INSP TYPE CATEGORY $REMITTED  EMPESTAB
CITY            STATE ZIP    CLOSECONF OPT REPT# SCOPE    OWNERSHIP  EMPINSP    LWDI
COUNTY (NAME/CODE)           CASE CLSD PREV ACT UNION     CLASS      EMPCNTRL
                            RELTD ACT
```

		GR		ABT				INITIAL	CURRENT	C SETTLM-T HAZD
	CITATION	RE ISSUANCE ABATE	CMP	INITIAL	CURRENT	F-T-A	F-T-A	N DISPOS-N SUBS
STANDARD	TYP IDENT VC	DATE	DATE CDE	PENALTY	PENALTY	PENALTY	PENALTY	T /FINORDT CODE

```
********************************
OCCIDENTAL CHEMICAL CO-SUWANNE 0419700   013608617    *** CONTINUED ***
      19101000 C            O 010018    8/12/80 9/16/80 N      0        0         0        0
      19101000 E            O 01001C    8/12/80 2/16/81 N      0        0         0        0
********************************
OCCIDENTAL CHEMICAL CO-SUWANNE 0419700   013676994 G4860-C  2874
US 41 4 MILES NORTH ON C137   6/02/80  PR-PLANND SAFETY       0      2100
White Springs      FL 32096   6/04/80  151085300 PARTIAL            746
Hamilton           047       12/05/80  (NONE)    UNION    SPG-MFG   2100
                            R909062200

      1910.178 P01           O 01001    6/18/80 6/03/80 N      0        0         0        0
      1910.309 B   071010    O 01002    6/18/80 6/04/80 N      0        0         0        0
      1910.243 C03           O 01003    6/18/80 6/02/80 N      0        0         0        0
      1910.024 F             O 01004    6/18/80 6/21/80 N      0        0         0        0
      1910.110 B06   VI      O 01005    6/18/80 6/21/80 N      0        0         0        0
      1910.106 E02   IVD     O 01006    6/18/80 6/21/80 N      0        0         0        0
      1910.106 E06   II      O 01007    6/18/80 6/21/80 N      0        0         0        0
      1910.309 B   045023    O 01008    6/18/80 8/21/80 N      0        0         0        0
********************************
OCCIDENTAL CHEMICAL CO         0419700   013677018 G4860-C  2874
10 MILES N ON US RTE 41        6/05/80  PR-PLANND SAFETY       0      2100
White Springs      FL 32096    6/05/80  151085500 PARTIAL            250
Hamilton           047         6/20/80  (NONE)    UNION    SPG-MFG   2100

      1910.212 A03   II      O 01001    6/18/80 6/21/80 K      0        0         0        0
********************************
OCCIDENTAL CHEMICAL CO DIVISIO 0419700   013698956 K4370-C  2874
SUWANNEE RIVER COMPLEX         7/30/80  UN-FOLLOW SAFETY       0      2000
White Springs      FL 32096    7/30/80  151012400 PARTIAL             50
Hamilton           047         3/10/84  (NONE)    UNION              2000
********************************
OCCIDENTAL CHEMICAL CO DIVISIO 0419700   013623806 B6973-C  2819
SUWANNEE RIVER COMPLEX        10/15/81  UN-CMPLNT SAFETY       0       750
White Springs      FL 32096   10/16/81  151020900 PARTIAL              4
Hamilton           047        10/22/81  (NONE)    UNION               750
                            C320909708
```

124

```
ESTABLISHMENT INSPECTED      REPORT ID ACTIVITY# CSHO      SIC1/SIC2
ADDRESS                      OPEN DATE INSP TYPE CATEGORY  $REMITTED  EMPESTAB
CITY             STATE ZIP   CLOSECONF OPT REPT# SCOPE     OWNERSHIP  EMPINSP   LWDI
COUNTY (NAME/CODE)           CASE CLSD PREV ACT  UNION     CLASS      EMPCNTRL
                             RELTD ACT

                                          GR                ABT                INITIAL   CURRENT   C SETTLM-T HAZD
                             CITATION     RE ISSUANCE ABATE CMP INITIAL CURRENT F-T-A    F-T-A     N DISPOS-N SUBS
         STANDARD            TYP  IDENT  VC  DATE     DATE CDE PENALTY PENALTY PENALTY   PENALTY   T /FINORDT CODE
```

```
********************************
OCCIDENTAL CHEMICAL CO-SUWANNE 0419700  013665377 G2256-I  2874
COUNTY RD 137                  1/21/82  UN-CMPLNT HEALTH     O         2105
White Springs        FL 32069  1/21/82  151006000 PARTIAL             5
Hamilton             047       3/10/84  (NONE)    UNION               2105
                               C320910243
********************************
OCCIDENTAL CHEMICAL CO         0419700  001687854 L4398-I  2874
HWY 41                         3/22/84  UN-CMPLNT HEALTH     D         264
White Springs        FL 32096  3/26/84  000000157 PARTIAL  PRIV SEC   32        .61
Hamilton             047       3/26/84  (NONE)    UNION               10000
                               C070097241
********************************
OCCIDENTAL CHEMICAL CO         0419700  019520188 L4398-I  2874
HWY 41                         3/22/84  UN-CMPLNT HEALTH     O         264
White Springs        FL 32096  NO ENTRY 151015700 PARTIAL             32
Hamilton             047       NO DATE  (NONE)    UNION               264
                               C070097241
********************************
OCCIDENTAL CHEMICAL COMPANY    0419700  002161883 M5201-C  2819
COUNTY ROAD 137                5/20/85  PR-PLANND SAFETY     O         1900
White Springs        FL 32096  5/20/85  523-85    RECORDS  PRIV SEC   1900
Hamilton             047       5/20/85  1013660097 UNION   SPG-MFG    11000
********************************
OCCIDENTAL CHEMICAL CO.        0419700  100334945 C4361-C  2874
HIGHWAY #41                    10/31/85 UN-CMPLNT SAFETY     O         264
White Springs        FL 32096  11/01/85 705-85    PARTIAL  PRIV SEC   4
Hamilton             047       11/01/85 (NONE)    UNION    SPG-MFG    1000
                               C070542972
********************************
OCCIDENTAL CHEMICAL CO.        0419700  101632008 D2451-C  2874
HIGHWAY 41                     4/21/87  UN-CMPLNT SAFETY     O         1173
White Springs        FL 32096  4/21/87  498       PARTIAL  PRIV SEC   350
Hamilton             047       5/05/87  C070542253 UNION              1173
                               C070542253
```

```
ESTABLISHMENT INSPECTED          REPORT ID ACTIVITY# CSHO     SIC1/SIC2
ADDRESS                          OPEN DATE INSP TYPE CATEGORY $REMITTED  EMPESTAB
CITY            STATE ZIP  CLOSECONF OPT REPT# SCOPE   OWNERSHIP  EMPINSP   LWDI
COUNTY (NAME/CODE)         CASE CLSD PREV ACT  UNION   CLASS      EMPCNTRL
                           RELTD ACT
```

STANDARD	CITATION TYP	GR RE IDENT	VC	ISSUANCE DATE	ABATE DATE	ABT CMP CDE	INITIAL PENALTY	CURRENT PENALTY	INITIAL F-T-A PENALTY	CURRENT F-T-A PENALTY	C N T	SETTLM-T DISPOS-N /FINORDT	HAZD SUBS CODE

```
********************************
OCCIDENTAL CHEMICAL CORP.     0419700   017965708 G2256-I 2874
OFF STATE RD. 136, SWIFT CREEK 11/19/90 UN-CMPLNT HEALTH      0       260
White Springs     FL 32096 11/20/90       PARTIAL PRIV SEC            2
Hamilton          047      2/18/91  (NONE) UNION                     1700
                           C072463755

   OPT-INFO: N-16 ASBESTOS
********************************
OCCIDENTAL CHEMICALS CORPORATI 0419700   018347773 C1353-I 2873
COUNTY ROAD 137               4/02/91 UN-CMPLNT HEALTH      0       698
White Springs     FL 32096 4/02/91 118    PARTIAL PRIV SEC            4   2.72
Hamilton          047      5/09/91  (NONE) UNION                   245000
                           C073882847


          Total Inspections listed:    20
```

126

Sulfuric Acid Emissions

SCCC SPA EMISSIONS

ESTIMATE OF SULFUR DIOXIDE EMITTED PER YEAR FOR 1989, 1990, AND 1991

DATA		LIQUID FEED		LIQUID PRODUCT		P2O5 TONS PER YEAR
		P2O5	SO4	P2O5	SO4	
1989		54.02	2.76	70.16	3.13	425000
1990		54.47	3.00	70.19	3.34	435000
1991		54.64	3.29	69.81	3.63	440000
AVG.		54.38	3.02	70.05	3.37	433333

CALCULATION

THE DIFFERENCE BETWEEN THE PRODUCT AND FEED SO4 TO P2O5 RATIO REPRESENTS THE LOSS TO THE GAS STREAM.

	RATIO	
FEED	SO4/P2O5=	0.0555
PRODUCT	SO4/P2O5=	0.0481
	DIFFERENCE=	0.0074 TON OF SO4/TON OF P2O5

CONVERT SULFATE(SO4) TO SULFUR DIOXIDE(SO2)

.0074 X 64 M.W. SO2/ 96 M.W. SO4=   0.0049 TON OF SO2/TON OF P2O5

MULTIPLY THE GAS STREAM RATIO (.0049 T-SO2/T-P2O5) BY THE AVERAGE PRODUCTION TONNAGE PER YEAR

0.0049 TON OF SO2/TON OF P2O5   X   433333 P2O5 TON /YEAR=   2,123 TONS OF SO2/YEAR

OR   4,246,663 LBS OF SO2 /YEAR

Occidental Exposures: Gary's Story

Earth Island Journal - Winter/Spring 1999

by George C. Glasser

Gary Pittman's first and last job was working for the Occidental Chemical Corporation's phosphoric acid factories in Hamilton County, Florida. Gary was 18 and in excellent health when he started to work as a sample man in the analytical laboratory of the corporation's Suwannee River Plant. He rose to supervising one-third of Occidental's Swift Creek plant, earning about $50,000 a year.

Today, Gary is unable to work. He suffers from autoimmune disorders, toxic myopathy, chronic obstructive lung disease with emphysema, chronic bronchitis, blood disorders, chronic fatigue syndrome, liver dysfunctions, polyarthritis, swelling of feet and lower legs, muscle weakness, cardiac arrhythmia, memory loss and reactive depression. He walks with a waddling gait and suffers dizziness. The diagnosis: Toxic Brain Syndrome.

While Gary and his coworkers worked amid toxic, corrosive fumes, Occidental Chemical's corporate elite sat safely in air-conditioned offices seven miles from the factory.

Sometimes, the concentrated airborne acidic cocktails at the Occidental plants would eat the paint off cars and etch windshields. Secretaries sent to the plant on errands complained of their pantyhose being dissolved.

Through the years, Occidental's management assured everyone that they were only being exposed to harmless chemicals. The truth was that both the employees and the nearby population were being exposed to highly toxic chemicals and radioactive pollution.

A History of Hazards

In anticipation of a 20 percent increase in the global demand for superphosphate fertilizer, chemical corporations have dumped more than $10 billion into phosphoric acid and phosphate mining in the state of Florida. Along with orange juice, phosphoric acid and superphosphate fertilizer are Florida's primary exports.

The adverse environmental and health effects of phosphoric acid production have been well-documented since the 1970's. The Environmental Protection Agency (EPA) has set standards for exposure to the industry's phosphate pollutants and the Occupational Safety and Health Administration (OSHA) has established strict safety requirements for workers. But to the author's knowledge, neither the EPA nor the Centers for Disease Control (CDC) has ever commissioned any substantive health-safety studies on the risks of exposure to pollutants resulting from phosphoric acid production.

Gypsum stacks piled high with production wastes, exhaust from cooling stacks and wastewater ponds are the primary local source s of air and groundwater pollutants, particularly hydrogen fluoride. Hydrogen fluoride combines with water to produce hydrofluoric acid, the most corrosive acid known. Hydrofluoric acid will react with most anything - including glass - to form fluorides.

According to a 1987 article in the Florida Scientist by the late Howard Moore, in the presence of moisture, a series of reactions between suspended solids and hydrogen fluoride can create pollutants that can be blown hundreds of miles from their source.

These airborne fluorides can be very reactive. When inhaled, many fluoride salts react with moist lung tissue, breaking down into hydrofluoric acid and other components. Inside the lungs, hydrofluoric acid burns tiny holes in the tissue and deposits silica and toxic metals at the site.

Phyllis Mullenix, a pioneer researcher on the neurotoxic effects of fluorides, has said that inhaling toxic fluoride compounds is "like giving them running shoes." As soon as they enter a living system, they begin to cause damage.

According to Dr. Gary Lyman of the University of South Florida Medical Center, people living near phosphate fertilizer plants are twice as likely to develop lung cancer and osteoblastic leukemia. While these high cancer rates among people living near phosphoric acid plants have been noted, little has been said about workers and their families. These workers are at ground zero. They are the ones that have to go into acid reaction vessels filled with toxic fumes and scour radioactive gypsum scale from filters and walls.

This scale is so radioactive (up to 100,000 picocuries of radium per gram) that the only landfill in the country that accepts naturally occurring radioactive wastes will not accept it. Instead, the radioactive wastes are buried in the gypsum stacks or dumped into holding ponds.

Crystallized, radioactive silica tetrafluoride build up is so hard and encrusted, it has to be chipped away with jack hammers. They also had to beat the water circulation pipes with hammers and run over them with trucks to dislodge the silica tetrafluoride. This maintenance was only done when the Florida Department of Environmental Protection, the EPA or OSHA had given notification that an inspection of the facilities was about to take place.

Industry's Pollution: America's Fluoridation

The fluorosilicic acid produced inside a phosophorous plant's pollution scrubbers is sold as a water fluoridation agent. Despite the fact that more than 50 percent of US cities that fluoridate use some form of this industrial waste in municipal drinking water, neither the EPA nor the Public Health Service can produce one clinical study vouching for the safety of the substance.

The plants also produce the sulfuric acid that is essential to phosphoric acid production. When the acid is mixed with finely ground phosphate rock, it produces vapors that contain heavy metals, sulfates, fluorosilicates, hydrogen fluoride and other contaminants. Uncontrolled releases of toxic hydrogen sulfide gas are common in the vicinity of these plants.

In 1995, the Florida Department of Environmental Protection (FDEP) required all phosphate fertilizer producers to install vinyl lining under new gypsum stacks. The action was taken to prevent new gypsum stacks from leaching contaminants into the already polluted local aquifers. Unfortunately, the vinyl liners were only a feel good measure as they do nothing to prevent runoff from the stacks or to prevent air pollution.

The EPA originally forced manufacturers to install pollution scrubbers in the late 1960s and early 1970s, but both the EPA and FDEP have tended to turn a blind eye to violations.

Phosphate rock contains Uranium-238. During the post-WW2 and Cold War eras, 75 percent of the uranium oxide used to produce nuclear weapons and fuel came from several Florida phosphate fertilizer plants. EPA's laxity may be a leftover attitude from the days when phosphate fertilizer plants were a national security asset.

Pittman's Day in Court

In 1997,. Pittman and seven other former Occidental employees filed a suit against the Occidental Chemical Corporation for battery, fraud and deceit, anti-pollution statutes and intentional infliction of emotional distress. Pittman's deposition reads like a 20-year sentence in Hell. "When I first started working for Occidental," Pittman recalled, "safety considerations were basically nonexistent. The only thing we were required to wear were safety glasses. Gloves, respirators and dust masks weren't furnished.

"I remember one incident when I was assigned the task of cleaning the filter hood and the pollution scrubber. Powdery fluorosilicate dust was everywhere. As we were cleaning, the fluorosilicate dust covered us, and it was very hot; we were sweating profusely. When the fluorosilicate dust mixed with the perspiration, it would form fluorosilicic acid on the skin and blister us if we did not wash it off.

"I remember going home after one episode in the pollution scrubber. I started coughing and choking. My eyes started to burn. I realized that my clothes were fuming. I rolled the window down in my truck so I could see to drive home. Reaching home, I removed my clothes and gave them to my wife to wash. Well, the only things that came out of the washing machine intact were the zipper and a couple of buttons."

"It wasn't uncommon to develop acid sores, rashes and blisters after those jobs. It also wasn't uncommon to cough up blood after breathing the fluorosilicates and other fumes."

The fluorosilicates found in pollution scrubbers contain heavy metals and radionuclides including radium-226, radon-222 and uranium-238. Silicon tetra fluoride is a highly toxic fluoride compound. The autopsy of a man who died from several minutes' exposure to concentrated fumes at a phosphate fertilizer plant revealed a coating of silica on his lungs. The cause of death, however, was fluorine poisoning.

Gary also has emphysema and classic symptoms of silicosis. In the phosphate industry, the older workers refer to the condition as "chemical pneumonia."

Most manufacturers require employee urine tests to track levels of chemical- exposure as a basic risk-management protection against future lawsuits. But in his 20 years of working for Occidental, Gary never had a urine test, even when he became ill.

In 1987, according to Gary who was then a supervisor at the facility, Occidental shut down a pollution scrubber, stating that it was no longer needed. Gary's claim has been substantiated by fellow employees. For almost three years - in violation of state regulations and the US Clean Air Act - Occidental operated with the scrubber shut down to save the cost of maintenance and electric power to the pumps. As a result, according to Pittman, the entire population of Hamilton County and surrounding North Florida was exposed to toxic emissions. Occidental's workers were exposed to even higher levels.

Poisoned, Fired and Ignored

With each episode of illness, Gary would leave work and his health would improve. But after returning to work, the symptoms would return - a textbook scenario of exposure to workplace toxins.

By 1993, after almost 21 years of workplace exposure, Gary was totally incapacitated. Unable to walk up a flight of stairs, he was laid off by Occidental management. Pittman claims that he was never offered a less taxing position and was not allowed to return to work.

None of the doctors treating Gary ever explored his workplace exposure to carbon tetrachloride, barium chlorides, hydrogen fluoride, fluorosilicates, sulfates, potassium cyanide, chemical solvents or other damaging and carcinogenic chemicals. Early diagnoses of Pittman's condition included degenerative muscle disease, AIDS, Lyme disease and nonspecific myopathy.

Gary was never tested for industrial toxics until he visited the Environmental Health Center in Dallas, Texas. The Center diagnosed toxic brain syndrome after reviewing Gary's previous medical records and a brain spectrograph that showed neurological damage typical of exposure to neurotoxins and heavy metals.

Numerous Occidental employees all suffer from similar medical problems - including two other plaintiffs in the lawsuit. According to Gary, employees in the processing plants "seemed to stay sick all the time. It was like they had a cold or the flu all the time. They were always taking over-the-counter medications so they could keep working." He names people with heart arrhythmias and symptoms of toxic brain syndrome, and stomach, lung, brain and bone cancers, leukemia and benign brain tumors.

Employees were also exposed to contaminants in the plant's drinking water. Gary suspected that wastewater from the holding ponds was leaching into the aquifer. Fluoride levels in the water were found to be 15 to 17 parts per million -. four times the EPA's permissible level. Phosphoric acid levels in the water were also very high. The drinking water was so laden with corrosive chemicals that the metal pipes eventually crumbled.

The drinking water became so contaminated that the employees complained it was undrinkable. A reverse osmosis system was installed but contaminants soon clogged the system and rendered it ineffective. After that, many employees brought their own water, or drank soft drinks.

A complaint written by Pittman's attorneys alleges that Occidental failed to provide and/or destroyed product-data safety sheets and removed warning labels on toxic chemicals to avoid purchasing adequate safety equipment. Occidental has made no public comment regarding this complaint.

Pittman states that ventilation in the work areas was poor and that safety equipment often failed. "We poured all sorts of chemicals down an open drain in the floor. Sometimes they would start boiling and fuming. All those noxious fumes were recirculated by the air conditioning system. We were continuously breathing that stuff. Back then, we didn't know any better."

The complaint submitted by two Jacksonville, Florida law firms - Coker, Myres, Schickel, Sorenson and Higgenbottom and Boyer, Tanzler and Boyer - states: "Not only did the Defendants fail to provide adequate and operational ventilation, but also, to further reduce costs, the Defendants, even on occasion when the toxic fume stacks were fully operational, simply turned them off."

Occidental ignored the most fundamental recommendations for worker safety with regard to toxic chemicals and fluorine as spelled out in the Public Health Service/Centers for Disease Control publication, Occupational Diseases: A Guide to their Recognition: "Attention should be given promptly to any burns from fluorine compounds due to absorption of the fluorine at the burn site." Gary and his coworkers were never afforded any medical attention nor were they provided with adequate protective equipment.

Of the eight original plaintiffs, two have died: One, a nonsmoker, died of lung and liver cancer;the other died of bone cancer.

"I read in the paper that studies… showed that Hamilton County has the highest cancer rate in Florida. Columbia and Suwannee Counties also have very high cancer rates compared to other counties in Florida. Those counties are right next to Hamilton," Pittman relates. "I wondered, why here? Hamilton County is basically a rural, farming county. You would think the air is less contaminated. The overall environment is cleaner. You would think the people would be healthier than in the big cities. The only thing here that is not in some of the other counties is Occidental Chemical Company.

Pittman thought about reporting the illegal emissions to Florida Department of Environmental Protection, OSHA and the EPA. But, he decided, what good would it do to report the problem "to the people who already know what is going on. They know people are sick and dying because of Occidental. If they were really concerned and cared about the public, they would have done something about Occidental a long time ago."

Gary Owen Pittman knows that he is going up against a mammoth organization with much to lose. The parent company of Occidental Chemical Corporation's parent, Hooker Chemical Corporation, is no stranger to litigation. Hooker was responsible for Love Canal. (Both companies are owned by the parent company Occidental Petroleum Corp.)

"It's hard for us to trust anyone after what we've been through. I know Occidental has the power to buy and intimidate people. They could even cause my lawyers problems. They give money to political candidates, and I imagine they help the judges who think their way to get elected is to be friendly toward Occidental. All of us know that we're alone and can't depend on anyone, except one another.

Originally published in the Sarasota ECO Report Summer 1996

Fluoride and the Phosphate Connection

Earth Island Journal Special Feature - **Fluorides and the Environment**

Summer/Fall 1997

by George C. Glasser

Cities all over the US purchase hundreds of thousands of gallons of fresh pollution concentrate from Florida - fluorosilicic acid (H_2SiF_6) - to fluoridate water.

Fluorosilicic acid is composed of tetrafluorosiliciate gas and other species of fluorine gases captured in pollution scrubbers and concentrated into a 23% solution during wet process phosphate fertilizer manufacture. Generally, the acid is stored in outdoor cooling ponds before being shipped to US cities to artificially fluoridate drinking water.

Fluoridating drinking water with recovered pollution is a cost-effective means of disposing of toxic waste. The fluorosilicic acid would otherwise be classified as a hazardous toxic waste on the Superfund Priorities List of toxic substances that pose the most significant risk to human health and the greatest potential liability for manufacturers.

Phosphate fertilizer suppliers have more than $10 billion invested in production and mining facilities in Florida. Phosphate fertilizer production accounts for $800 million in wages per year. Florida's mines produce 30% of the world supply and 75% of the US supply of phosphate fertilizers. Much of the country's supply of fluorosilicic acid for water fluoridation is also produced in Florida.

Phosphate fertilizer manufacturing and mining are not environment friendly operations. Fluorides and radionuclides are the primary toxic pollutants from the manufacture of phosphate fertilizer in Central Florida. People living near the fertilizer plants and mines, experience lung cancer and leukemia rates that are double the state average. Much of West Central Florida has become a toxic waste dump for phosphate fertilizer manufacturers. Federal and state pollution regulations have been modified to accommodate phosphate fertilizer production and use: These regulations have included using recovered pollution for water fluoridation.

Radium wastes from filtration systems at phosphate fertilizer facilities are among the most radioactive types of naturally occurring radioactive material (NORM) wastes. The radium wastes are so concentrated, they cannot be disposed of at the one US landfill licensed to accept NORM wastes, so manufacturers dump the radioactive wastes in acidic ponds atop 200-foot-high gypsum stacks. The federal government has no rules for its disposal.

During the late 1960s, fluorine emissions were damaging crops, killing fish and causing crippling skeletal fluorosis in livestock. The EPA became concerned and enforced regulations requiring manufacturers to install pollution scrubbers. At that time, the facilities were dumping the concentrated pollution directly into waterways leading into Tampa Bay.

A Phosphate Worse than Death

In the late 1960s, EPA chemist Ervin Bellack worked out the ideal solution to a monumental pollution problem. Because recovered phosphate fertilizer manufacturing waste contain about 19% fluorine, Bellack concluded that the concentrated "scrubber liquor" could be a perfect water fluoridation agent. It was a liquid and easily soluble in water, unlike sodium fluoride - a waste product from aluminum manufacturing. It was also inexpensive.

Fate also intervened. The aluminum industry, which previously supplied sodium fluoride for water fluoridation, was facing a shortage of fluorspar used in smelting aluminum. Consequently, there was a shortage of sodium fluoride to fluoridate drinking water.

For the phosphate fertilizer industry, the shortage of sodium fluoride was the key to turning red ink into black and an environmental liability into a perceived asset. With the help of the EPA, fluorosilicic acid was transformed from a concentrated toxic waste and a liability into a "proven cavity fighter."

The EPA and the US Public Health Service waived all testing procedures and - with the help of the American Dental Association (ADA) - encouraged cities to add the radioactive concentrate into America's drinking water as an "improved" form of fluoride.

The product is not "fluorine" or "fluoride" as proponents state: It is a pollution concentrate. Fluorine is only one captured pollutant comprising about 19% of the total product.

By 1983, the official EPA policy was expressed by EPA Office of Water Deputy Administrator Rebecca Hanmer as follows: "In regard to the use of fluosilicic (fluorosilicic) acid as a source of fluoride for fluoridation, this agency regards such use as an ideal environmental solution to a long-standing problem. By recovering by-product fluosilicic acid from fertilizer manufacturing, water and air pollution are minimized, and water utilities have a low-cost source of fluoride available to them."

A Hot New Property

In promoting the use of the pollution concentrate as a fluoridation agent, the ADA, Federal agencies and manufacturers failed to mention that it was radioactive. Whenever uranium is found in nature as a component of a mineral, a host of other radionuclides are always found in the mineral in various stages of decay. Uranium and all of its decay-rate products are found in phosphate rock, fluorosilicic acid and phosphate fertilizer.

During wet-process manufacturing, trace amounts of radium and uranium are captured in the pollution scrubber. This process was the subject of an article by H.F. Denzinger, H. J. König and G.E. Krüger in the fertilizer industry journal, Phosphorus & Potassium (No. 103, Sept./Oct. 1979) discussed how radionuclides are carried into the fluorosilicic acid.

While the uranium and radium in fluorosilicic acid are known carcinogens, two decay products of uranium are even more carcinogenic: radon-222 and polonium-210.

During the acidulation process that creates phosphoric acid, radon gas contained in the phosphate pebble can be released in greater proportions than other decay-rate products (radionuclides) and carried over into the fluorosilicic acid. Polonium may also be captured in greater quantities during scrubbing operations because, like radon, it can readily combine with fluoride.

In written communications to the author, EPA Office of Drinking Water official Joseph A. Cotruvo and Public Health Service fluoridation engineer Thomas Reeves have acknowledged the presence of radionuclides in fluorosilicic acid.

Radon-222 is not an immediate threat because it stops emitting alpha radiation and decays into lead-214 in 3.86 days. Lead-214 appears to be harmless but it eventually decays into bismuth-214 and then into polonium-214. Unless someone knew to look for specific isotopes, no one would know that a transmutation into the polonium isotope had occurred.

Polonium-210, a decay product of bismuth-210, has a half-life of 138 days and gives off intense alpha radiation as it decays into regular lead and becomes stable. Any polonium-210 that might be present in the phosphate concentrate could pose a significant health threat. A very small amount of polonium-210 can be very dangerous, giving off 5,000 times more alpha radiation than the same amount of radium. As little as 0.03 microcuries (6.8 trillionths of a gram) of polonium-210 can be carcinogenic to humans.

The lead isotope behaves like calcium in the body. It may be stored in the bones for years before turning into polonium-210 and triggering a carcinogenic release of alpha radiation.

Drinking water fluoridated with fluorosilicic acid contains radon at every sequence of its decay to polonium. The fresher the pollution concentrate, the more polonium it will contain.

As long as the amount of contaminants added to the drinking water (including radionuclides in fluorosilicic acid) do not exceed the limits set forth in the Safe Drinking Water Act, the EPA has no regulatory problem with the use of any contaminated products for drinking water treatment.

Big Risks: No Tests

Despite the increased cancer risk from using phosphate waste to fluoridate drinking water, the EPA nor the Centers for Disease Control have never commissioned or required any clinical studies with the pollution concentrate - specifically, the hexafluorsilicate radical whose toxicokinetic properties are different than the lone, fluoride ion.

Section 104 (I) (5) of the Comprehensive Environmental Response, Compensation and Liability Act (CERCLA) directs the Toxic Substances and Disease Registry, the EPA, the Public Health Service and the National Toxicology Program to initiate a program of research on fluoride safety. However, after almost 30 years of using fluorosilicic acid and sodium fluorosilicate to fluoridate the drinking water, not one study has been commissioned.

The fluoride ion only hypothetically exists as an entity in an ideal solution of purified water - and tap water is far from pure H2O. All clinical research with animal models is done using 99.97% pure sodium fluoride and double distilled or deionized water. Among the thousands of clinical studies about fluoride, not one has been done with the pollution concentrate or typical tap water containing fluorides.

Synergy Soup

The fluorosilicic acid is also contaminated with small traces of arsenic, cadmium, mercury, lead, sulfates, iron and phosphorous, not to mention radionuclides. Some contaminants have the potential to react with the hexafluorosilicate radical and may act as complex ionic compounds. The biological fates and toxicokinetic properties of these complex ions are unknown.

The reality of artificial water fluoridation is so complex that determining the safety of the practice may be impossible. Tap water is chemically treated with chlorine, soluble silicates, phosphate polymers and many other chemicals. In addition, the source water itself may contain a variety of contaminants.

The addition of a fluoridation agent can create synergized toxicants in a water supply that have unique toxicokinetic properties found only in that particular water supply. Consequently, any maladies resulting from chronic ingestion of the product likely would be dismissed as a local or regional anomaly unrelated to water fluoridation.

Technically, artificially fluoridating drinking water is a violation of the Safe Drinking Water Act (SDWA). Under statutes of the SDWA, federal agencies are forbidden from endorsing, supporting, requiring or funding the practice of adding any chemicals to the water supply other than for purposes of water purification. However, the Public Health Service (PHS) applies semantics to circumvent Federal law in order to promote and fund the practice.

PHS states that they only recommend levels of fluorides in the drinking water, and it is the sole decision of a state or community to fluoridate drinking water.

Federal agencies are forbidden from directly funding or implementing water fluoridation but Federal Block Grants are given to States to use as they see fit. Through second and third parties (such as the American Dental Association, state health departments and state fluoridation coordinators), PHS encourages communities to apply for Federal Block Grant funds to implement fluoridation.

The legality of using of Federal Block Grant funds to fund water fluoridation, a practice prohibited by Federal law, has never been addressed in the courts.

Vendors selling the pollution concentrate as a fluoridation agent use a broad disclaimer found on the Material Data Safety Sheet that states:

- *"no responsibility can be assumed by vendor for any damage or injury resulting from abnormal use, from any failure to adhere to recommended practices, or from any hazards inherent to the product."*

The next time you turn on the tap and water gushes out into a glass, reflect on the following disclaimer from the EPA's 1997 Fluoride: Regulatory Fact Sheet:

- *"In the United States, there are no Federal safety standards which are applicable to additives, including those for use in fluoridating drinking water."*

George Glasser is a Florida-based writer whose work has appeared in Newlife, Whole Life Times, the Sarasota ECO Report and the Tampa Tribune.

Gary O. Pittman
Rt. 1, Box 85-A
Jennings, FL 32053
Tel: 904-792-3975
email: gop@alltel.net
November 18, 1998

Dear Congressman or Senator:

I worked in the phosphate fertilizer industry for about twenty-one years. My last position was supervising one-third of the evaporation and purification processes at the Occidental Chemical Corporation, Swift Creek Chemical Complex. That position required a thorough knowledge of almost every facet of producing phosphoric acid for fertilizer and animal feed supplement.

Today, I am disabled and suffer from toxic brain syndrome, emphysema, heart arrhythmias and other health problems due to chemical exposure. Many of my co-workers also suffer from similar illnesses. Of the eight original people in my support group, two are dead from cancers. One man had lung and liver cancer, and the second man died from myeloma (bone cancer); neither man had ever smoked and seldom, if ever, consumed alcoholic beverages according to their wives and friends. Another man has leukemia which is presently in remission. Many of my co-workers have developed brain cancers/tumors and stomach cancers. Myopathy, arthritis, liver dysfunctions, lung problems, symptoms of toxic brain syndrome, etc. are also very common health problems among my co-workers and myself. Toxic brain syndrome and heart problems seem to be the most common problems among the workers. Hamilton County also has the highest rate of cancer in Florida due to pollution from phosphoric acid manufacturing.

The doctors at Shands Hospital, Gainesville, FL (specializing in cancer research and treatment) said that the type of lung and liver cancer one man died from were unidentifiable; they had never seen it before.

You might say that I should be contacting my own U.S. Representative and Senator because this is a regional problem, and it is not in your back yard. However, this is not the case. We were exposed to the same chemicals that the *USEPA and U.S. Centers for Disease Control and Prevention* recommend as fluoridation agents to fluoridate the drinking water for over 100,000,000 people. It is likely that your constituents are consuming the pollution, and you might be drinking it because Washington, D.C. is fluoridated.

Over 50% of the communities in the United States use fluorosilicic acid (H_2SiF_6) or sodium fluorosilicate (Na_2SiF_6) to fluoridate drinking water. Neither the *USEPA nor U.S. Centers for Disease Control and Prevention* can provide one safety study proving the product is safe for long-term, low-level consumption. Not one clinical study with animal models has ever been done with the products.

Both fluorosilicic acid (FSA) and sodium fluorosilicate (SFS) are derived from pollution scrubbing operations from phosphoric acid production. The pollution scrubber liquor is a unique product derived from a specific process with unique toxicological characteristics. The presence of chlorides, amines, diesel fuel, kerosene, sulfides, reagents, metals (including arsenic, lead, aluminum, uranium-238 and its decay rate products, etc.), phosphorus and other toxic reactants create a specific product in which FSA is the active ingredient. FSA only comprises about 23% of the total pollution concentrate. It is a highly corrosive acid which can react with most organic and inorganic substances to form many different complexes and possibly very toxic fluorides. I state again, not one safety study has been done with these particular products.

There are many factors involved in the creation of the FSA. Once an insight is gained about how the phosphoric acid is made, the FSA becomes even more frightening. Other chemicals are added such as oil based defoamers (possibly containing dioxins), polymers, petroleum products, naphthalene, chlorides, sulfides, Synspar and various reagents. During the phosphoric acid concentration processes, these added chemicals and inherent toxic contaminants common in phosphate rock are boiled off the acid in a partial vacuum at very high temperatures, about 500 degrees F. The vapors from all these chemicals are washed and captured in the pollution scrubbers along with the fluorine and fluorosilicate gases.

Although it is more convenient for scientists to believe the pollution scrubbing is discriminate, it is not. One scrubber catches all, including pollution from tank farms and other processes. Also, the more efficient the scrubbing operation, the more contaminants will be concentrated in the scrubber liquor.

Phosphoric acid reaction vessels are made of the alloy, Hastelloy G-30. The Hastelloy G-30 vessels only last for about three years before they are tossed or rebuilt. Each vessel costs about $1,000,000. The vessels are corroded beyond use by the presence of fluorides and chlorides in the phosphoric acid. The metals from Hastelloy G-30 (nickel, beryllium, etc.) are also present in the FSA as metal complexed fluorosilicates.

Sulfuric acid is produced at these facilities, and the spent vanadium pentoxide catalyst, production sludge and waste water are dumped into the evaporation (settling) ponds. Evaporation ponds are the catch-all for almost all toxic wastes. Radioactive scale from reaction vessels and filters, phosphoric acid sludges, radioactive fluorosilicates chipped from scrubbing pads and chambers, and general toxic wastes are tossed into the mix.

To make matters worse, evaporation pond water is always used in the pollution scrubbers because there are strict regulations regarding fresh water usage in Florida. Most of the waste water, sludges and waste chemicals from the analytical labs are dumped into the evaporation ponds which is reused in production and/or to make the FSA for water fluoridation.

At this point, I believe it is evident that we are not dealing with a simple, pure, reagent grade SFA/SFS purchased from the chemical supply house as most researchers/chemists find it convenient to believe and predicate their hypotheses and research upon. If the captured pollution had no fluorides present, it would be dangerous to put in the water, but with the complex chemical reactions and possible reactions with both organic and inorganic compounds, FSA/SFS are very dangerous and carcinogenic/neurotoxic, as I well know.

This scenario is well beyond some laboratory chemist or researcher placing a few drops of reagent grade FSA or SFS into a flask of distilled water to make a "theoretical determination." It is not the same product.

The most frightening aspect is that no two batches are the same, and the toxic effects can vary from batch to batch. There would also be a variance from company to company supplying the product because of the type/grades of chemicals, quality of the phosphate rock, processes and what kind of solvent extraction method is used to produce phosphoric (solvent extraction is not commonly used anymore unless uranium is being extracted from 23-34% phosphoric acid; the Synspar flux method is preferred today).

About 6.8 mg/liter of 23% FSA is added to the water to achieve fluoridation at 1.0 ppm. The FSA is an ingredient in a complex product, and because of the nature of the chemical in the product, complex interactions have to occur during manufacture, e.g. heat, negative atmospheric pressure, catalyzing effects due to contact with metal vessels and additives. Of the 6.8 mg/liter, 5.8 is contaminant-laden water. If the fluoride ion could be isolated, per se (again, this is highly unlikely with water fluoridation), the toxicological characteristics would in no way relate to present water fluoridation research which is done with a different, pharmaceutical grade product.

No one has any idea of what reactions will occur under heat and partial vacuum. All these chemicals including radionuclides and other heavy metals are in the FSA/SFS. Some of the chemicals used in the process are also known carcinogens and neurotoxic substances. FSA/SFS is a real "witches brew." The bottom line is: You cannot mix that many reactive chemicals together under conditions which inspire reactions and not create a product unique to any other fluoridation agent produced in another environment. Possibly many fluorides are created with unique toxicological characteristics that do not readily dissociate in water as stated by the EPA/CDC.

Interestingly, all the people who say this product is "safe" have no concept of how it is produced. They cannot produce one safety study using either FSA or SFS from the manufacture of phosphoric acid. However, all responsible Federal agencies say it is safe without any data to back up the statement (see EPA Fluoride: Regulatory Fact Sheet).

I know what I have shared with you goes against the grain of many dentists and doctors, and the Federal agencies promoting drinking water fluoridation. But I was employed in the production of phosphoric acid for twenty-one years. I worked in about every position and in every aspect of production from the analytical laboratory to pilot experimental projects, and my last position was supervising one-third of the Occidental Swift Creek Chemical Complex. I can assure you the FSA and SFS used to fluoridate drinking water contains much more than "fluoride" as EPA/CDC would have you believe.

For every 6,800 gallons of FSA, 5,800 gallons is toxic pollution (cost effective means to dump pollution). If a study were to be done with the actual product, I am sure the results would be terrifying. I believe my co-workers and myself are examples of what clinical research will produce in animals.

I would ask you to look into this situation, not so much for myself, because I am aware of what has caused my health problems, but for the people and the unborn children who will be poisoned from these toxic products being "dumped" into the water.

I know the fluorosilicic acid and sodium fluorosilicate pollution from phosphoric acid production can't be good for anyone. My co-workers and myself are examples of the harmful, toxic effects of these products; we were exposed to the same pollution that is dumped into much of America's drinking water as a fluoridation agent.

I respectfully request, for the health and well-being of future generations of Americans, that the use of fluorosilicic acid and derivatives for drinking water fluoridation be banned and more stringent environmental legislation be enacted regarding phosphoric acid production. I feel that it is your moral obligation to address these issues.

Sincerely,

Gary O. Pittman

Excerpts from the article Death in the Air (1999):
Wives' Comments

Gloria Pittman:

His wife, Gloria, said, "On February 9, 1993, Gary came home from work early. He was sick, vomiting and had an unbearable headache. Later that night, he was coughing up blood. He thought it was a virus, but no one else in the family had any symptoms.

"The next morning, I went into labour with our third child. Still, sick, poor Gary had to take me to the hospital. While I was giving birth to James, Gary was trying to survive in the waiting room. When he came in to see me and James, he looked like death. He didn't want to go home, but I told him I would be all right. I worried that he wouldn't be able to make it to the house. I thought he was going to die on the way home.

"Our doctor said that Gary had a muscle-destructive process and there was nothing he could do except refer him to a specialist. We went to the specialist with medical records in hand. After reviewing the results of Gary's blood tests, the specialist said that a muscle biopsy had to be done the same day. He said we couldn't wait because Gary was on the verge of death. The results confirmed that Gary had auto-immune disease and polymyositis (simultaneous inflammation of many muscles). The doctor said that if he could get the isoenzyme levels down, he could get the muscle disease under control. The only problem was that Gary would never be the same."

As time passed, Gary's condition worsened. Gloria said, "There were times when his feet and lower legs would swell so bad, Gary was bedridden for weeks at a time. The pain was intolerable. I remember hearing him talk to himself late at night and in the early morning. The only way he could go to the bathroom was by dragging himself across the floor. When he was that bad off, I would load the wheel-chair into the car. Gary's seventy-three year old father helped me carry him to the car and we drove to Gainesville. By the time we arrived at the doctor's office, Gary told me that his feet were so swollen that he couldn't feel the pain anymore. Sometimes, it looked as though his feet were about to rot off. They gave Gary steroids and pain killers."

Joann Nash

There was more than a touch of anger and bitterness in Joann Nash's voice as she recalled Jesse's last day at Occidental. "Back in June of 1996, after he had used all his vacation time visiting the Dallas Environmental Health

Center for toxicological testing, we finally found that Jesse's health problems were caused by chemical poisoning.

"He called the company and they told him to go out to the plant for a meeting with the human resources people. The meeting was held in a conference room where the group had been eating watermelon. They never bothered cleaning the mess from the conference room table where they sat to discuss Jesse's problem. I couldn't believe it! Jesse was so sure that the company was going to take care of him and help him get the proper treatment. All they offered Jesse was unpaid medical leave."

Charlotte Baldwin

Billy Baldwin's wife, Charlotte, spoke of his last day working for Occidental. "Billy was sick at his stomach, had headaches and was as white as a ghost. I tried to talk him into going to a doctor but he told me that if he took time off from work he would lose his job.

"When I came home from work November 13, 1993, Billy said that he couldn't take it anymore; he needed to see a doctor. I rushed him to the emergency room. He was immediately admitted for severe anaemia and stayed there for three days.

"The doctors at Lakeshore Hospital in Lake City, Florida ran a blood test and bone marrow biopsy. They said they couldn't find anything wrong with Billy.

"Billy's doctor prescribed a course of vitamin B12 and folic acid once a day for a year. When I went to get the medicine the pharmacist immediately asked who wrote the prescription. Then I asked what was wrong and the pharmacist said that athletes didn't take that much vitamin B12 and he would have to verify the prescription with the doctor.

"After two weeks on B12, Billy wasn't getting any better. His white blood cell count was rising. We were told to see a doctor in Gainesville, Florida.

"The doctor examined him and had blood drawn. After waiting several hours, he called us in and asked Billy how he managed to walk into the office with such a low red blood cell count.

"The doctor told me to take Billy to North Florida Hospital and be admitted. They gave him a transfusion of three units of blood and did a bone marrow biopsy. He said the results would take a few days.

"I answered the call from the hospital and handed Billy the telephone. The doctor told him to come to his office at nine the next morning because they needed to talk. I took the telephone and asked what was wrong. Reluctantly, the doctor told me that Billy had the leukaemia, the worst type. It broke my heart, but I never told Billy. I waited for the doctor to tell Billy because I couldn't bear to tell him such bad news."

Karen Hobby

Karen, the wife of Bobby Hobby, recalled his last days working at the phosphate complex: "In April 1996, we had an automobile accident. Two weeks later, Bobby's back began to hurt him. There were times he couldn't get up, but somehow he continued to work.

"Bobby finally went to his primary care doctor, who found only a few slipped disks. Eventually, he went to see a neurologist who found a broken vertebra. Because of the accident, the neurologist ordered a MRI scan. Still believing the injury was from the accident, he told us it was possible that the vertebra was broken and needed alignment.

"Two weeks later, we went back to the neurologist. We were not prepared for what he had to say. They discovered a tumor inside the bone and that is what caused the break. The doctor referred us to a specialist. After the consultation, Bobby was admitted into the hospital for a bone biopsy. They did a battery of tests including the bone biopsy; the diagnosis was Multiple Myeloma. The survival rate was about 2-3 years, and there was no cure.

"Bobby died in 1998."

—

Made in the USA
Las Vegas, NV
16 March 2025

19644422R00083